# Endorsements for The

As one responsible for forming our future priest evangelizers for the Church in the United States, I would highly encourage seminarians to read Fr. Mele's excellent work.

How often we preachers get frustrated because of our human limitations in preaching. Fr. Mele gives us excellent direction on how to keep our preaching fresh, lively and meaningful.

As a seminary rector, I am always concerned that what the seminarians learn in the classroom can be preached effectively, convincingly, and joyfully. This is a core element of evangelization. Fr. Mele provides us a practical reflection on how to keep our preaching evangelical.

With human lips and a human heart, Jesus revealed to us the mystery of himself, the Father, and the Holy Spirit. The preacher is called to make Christ and his Gospel accessible in the same manner. Fr. Mele helps preachers understand how to integrate the human, spiritual and theological dimensions of good preaching. As a seminary rector, I will encourage my seminarians to read this excellent reflection on preaching.

—Fr. James Wehner
Author, Rector-President of Notre Dame Seminary


The very core of the vocation of the priest is to proclaim the Gospel of Jesus Christ. This has been done well and not so well throughout the years. Fr. Mele lays out the history and the problems of Catholic preaching and then offers some very practical ways for the preacher to be God's Instrument of the Good News. Read this book and become the Instrument God is calling you to be!

—Fr. Larry Richards
Author, radio host, and Founder of
The Reason for Our Hope Foundation

Preaching for the new evangelization! From his experience as pastor and seminary rector, and drawing upon many years of responsibility for the pre-ordination and post-ordination formation of priests, Fr. Mele truly understands the challenges and the urgency of effectively preaching the Word of God in the twenty-first century. Seeing where we've come and where we are in today's world, he boldly points the direction for a "reform of the reform" of preaching, based on the pillars of Vatican II and the liturgical renewal. Fr. Mele gives the priest and deacon practical guidance on how to preach, and a deeper understanding of the task and opportunity the preacher faces in our times.

—Fr. Thomas Acklin
Author, Rector and Professor of Theology,
Saint Vincent Seminary

Fr. Mele, with the confident boldness that reminds one of the Spirit-filled preaching of the Acts of the Apostles, speaks to the fact that many homilies we hear at Sunday Mass do not lead us to a deeper encounter with Christ. His book, *The Sacred Conversation: The Art of Catholic Preaching and The New Evangelization,* holds our attention throughout by taking "into account the hopes and objectives of the Second Vatican Council, the struggles and needs of Catholics today, and the liturgical context in which homilies are preached." Not only seminary professors, priests, and deacons, but anyone who desires to enter more deeply into the mystery of the Eucharist will find Fr. Mele to be a trustworthy guide.

—Rt. Rev. Douglas R. Nowicki
Archabbot and Chancellor of Saint Vincent Archabbey,
College and Seminary

This book greatly broadens and deepens our understanding of the role of the homily in offering the Holy Sacrifice. In the Mass our Risen Lord makes himself available to us. Fr. Mele makes it clear that the basic function of the homily is to prepare us appropriately to respond to the divine initiative. Its task, in other words, is to call us to continuing conversion. The skill of any homilist who reads this book—and God grant it wide readership—is bound greatly to be enriched. And so will those to whom he proclaims the Gospel. As a homilist, I devoutly wish this book had fallen into my hands many years ago.

—Fr. Ray Ryland
Author, Chaplain of Catholics United for the Faith and
The Coming Home Network International

It is not often that a book on homiletics can be recommended for a general audience as well as the priest and deacons meant to learn from it. But I am giving Fr. Joseph Mele's *The Sacred Conversation* to friends that will never provide a homily in their lives. His steps for a "reform of the reform" of Catholic liturgical practices are inspiring to those of us who are in the pews, not just the pulpits.

Fr. Mele provides a sensible understanding of the liturgy—and the proper role of homiletics to the liturgy—that gives far more than a "how to" for a weekly sermon. A priest or deacon reading *The Sacred Conversation* will discover how "he must live the Gospel he preaches." The lay reader will find what all good homilies should accomplish—a book to shake us out of our complacency.

—Robert P. Lockwood
Author and national columnist for *Our Sunday Visitor*

Fr. Mele offers a reminder of the importance of sacred conversation as the heart of the Sunday homily. It is an invitation to the faith, to renewal, and to a grounded life situated within the Trinity, the institution of the Church, and the practices of the faith.

—Dr. Ronald C. Arnett
Chair and professor of the Department of
Communication & Rhetorical Studies and the Henry Koren,
C.S.Sp., Endowed Chair for
Scholarly Excellence at Duquesne University

This is more than a manual for good techniques. It's a recovery of the very purpose of liturgical preaching: to guide us into the divine mysteries. Fr. Mele has produced a manifesto for a Church alive with grace.

—Mike Aquilina
Author and Executive Vice President and Trustee of
St. Paul Center for Biblical Theology

"How can they call on him in whom they have not believed? And how can they believe in him of whom they have not heard? And how can they hear without someone to preach?" (Romans 10:14).

As Saint Paul points out, preaching and the preacher are central to evangelization. In *The Sacred Conversation* Fr. Joseph Mele has provided sound teaching on "the art of Catholic preaching." This fine book explains not only how to prepare the preaching but also how to form the preacher. It is both practical and inspirational.

If you are a priest, buy this book, read it, and keep it as a ready reference. If you are someone who knows a priest, buy it for him. Surely, it will bear fruit in the New Evangelization for those who apply its teaching.

—Regis J. Flaherty
Author and Director of the Gilmary retreat center

In his masterpiece, *The Ascent of Mount Carmel*, St. John of the Cross (1542–1591) said, "Although the preacher may speak remarkable truths, these will soon be forgotten since they do not enkindle the will." In the spirit of the Apostle Paul (1Corinthians 2:14), the saint agrees that the "rhetoric of human wisdom" must be subordinated to the manifestation of spirit and truth just as the love of learning must bow before the desire for God. This book fulfills the intentionality of scripture and the masters: it presents the art and discipline of *preaching* not only as a declaration of solid Church *teaching* but also as a way of *reaching* the hearts of every hearer. It is a timely book whose time has come.

—Dr. Susan Muto
Dean of Epiphany Academy of Formative Spirituality,
Pittsburgh, Pennsylvania

# The Sacred Conversation

## The Art of Catholic Preaching and The New Evangelization

Fr. Joseph Mele

EMMAUS
ROAD
PUBLISHING

Steubenville, Ohio
www.emmausroad.org

EMMAUS
ROAD
PUBLISHING

Emmaus Road Publishing
1468 Parkview Circle
Steubenville, Ohio 43952

Library of Congress Control Number: 2013936193
ISBN: 978-1-937155-97-1

Cover design and layout by Julie Davis, General Glyphics, Inc., Dallas, Texas

*Nihil Obstat*: Rev. Kris D. Stubna, S.T.D., Censor Librorum
Diocese of Pittsburgh

*Imprimatur*: Most Rev. David A. Zubik, DD, Bishop of Pittsburgh
April 8, 2013

The *nihil obstat* and *imprimatur* are official declarations that a work is considered to be free
from doctrinal or moral error. It is not implied that those who have granted same agree
with the content, opinions, or statements expressed.

# Dedication

Bishop John B. McDowell,
a dynamic and inspirational preacher and dear friend.

# Contents

# Foreword

*The Sacred Conversation: The Art of Catholic Preaching and the New Evangelization* could not come at a better time. The Church Universal has recently concluded the Synod on the New Evangelization and our Holy Father turns our attention to the mission of the Church today. At the same time, the United States bishops published the document, "Preaching the Mystery of Faith: The Sunday Homily," reminding all of us of the unique importance of the homily and its role in the New Evangelization. Now comes Father Joseph Mele's book which offers us welcome guidance as we try to see the challenge of Catholic preaching in the context of the New Evangelization.

The starting point for recognizing the value of this book is an understanding of the meaning and significance of the New Evangelization. The New Evangelization is a term that has become very familiar in the Church today. Blessed John Paul II began, more than three decades ago, to speak of the need for a new period of evangelization. He described it as announcement of the Good News about Jesus that is "new in ardor, method and expression" (Address to the Latin American Episcopal Conference (CELAM), March 9, 1983). Pope Benedict XVI has affirmed that the discernment of "the new demands of evangelization" is a "prophetic" task of the Supreme Pontiff (*Caritas in veritate*, 12). He emphasized that "the entire activity of the Church is an expression of love" that seeks to evangelize the world (*Deus caritas est*, 19).

At the Mass on Sunday, October 28, 2012 at Saint Peter's Basilica for the closing of the synod, Pope Benedict XVI reflected on some aspects of the New Evangelization. He spoke of the three areas and dimensions of the work of sharing and living the Gospel. The New Evangelization, he said, "applies, in the first instance, to the ordinary pastoral ministry that must be more animated by the fire of the Spirit." The second aspect of the New Evangelization, the Pope points out, is the Church's task "to evangelize, to proclaim the message of salvation to those who do not know Jesus Christ." This we traditionally refer to as the "*missio ad gentes*" or "mission to the nations." We all recall the terms "foreign missions" and "mission lands." The third aspect, the Pope notes in his homily, concerns "the baptized whose lives do not reflect the demands of baptism . . . the Church is particularly concerned that they should encounter Jesus Christ anew, rediscover the joy of faith and return to religious practice in the community of the faithful."

We are called to re-propose Christ as the answer to a world staggering under the weight of so many unanswered questions of the heart. We are called to be missionaries in the circumstances of our day with all of its challenges, within the context of the lives of the people who receive the message.

The New Evangelization requires an enthusiastic willingness to share the faith with a society greatly in need of it. Our challenge is to provide people with a new awareness and familiarity with Jesus—who is Love and Truth, and makes all things new—in practical language in the midst of their daily lives and concrete situations. Our duty is not just to announce, but to *adapt our approach* so as to attract and to urge an entire generation to find again the uncomplicated, genuine and tangible treasure of friendship with Jesus.

Preaching is at the heart of the New Evangelization. Jesus himself establishes evangelization as the very essence of the Church when he gives his disciples the commission to evangelize, that is, to announce this good news "to all the nations," (Mark 13:10; Luke 24:47) and to spread the Gospel by going forth "into the whole world "and to "proclaim the Gospel to every creature" (Mark 16:15; Matthew 28:19–20). The preaching spirit of the New Evangelization is captured in the Sermon on the Mount. We hear in Jesus' preaching an invitation to be connected to the vine of the Lord, eat of the bread of everlasting life and hear the words of truth, words that endure forever. Those ordained have a special task of transmitting faithfully and authoritatively the Gospel of Jesus Christ. It also falls to bishops, priests and deacons to call all of the evangelized to become evangelizers.

Brother to brother, Father Mele gently examines the state of Catholic preaching. On the one hand it is acknowledged that some of the dissatisfaction of Catholics with the state of preaching is justified and there is a real need for renewal and re-commitment to excellent preaching. On the other hand, it is also recognized that preaching becomes more and more challenging as we face a congregation who for two generations has been poorly catechized and lives in an increasingly secularized culture. Not to mention that the popularity of social media encourages important news to be shared in the space of a Facebook post or a 140 character "Tweet," making the kind of sustained attention and contemplative listening to the proclamation of the Word and homily harder and harder for many listeners.

What makes Father Mele's book so valuable is that it examines what influenced the decline in Catholic preaching and how it can be renewed, as well as lays the ground work for restoring the art of preaching by examining its relationship to the liturgy and to the hungering hearts of our people. With the experience of a seasoned preacher and the skill of a homiletics teacher, Father Mele uses his own extensive background to reflect on the discipline of crafting a homily. He rightly states that effective preaching begins with the spiritual life of the preacher. He writes "Who a priest is matters" (page 84). Preaching is a sacred responsibility made fruitful in the man who is humble, obedient, prayerful, and compassionate. Preachers are also invited to consider homily preparation and the way in which our homilies are delivered. For the priest new to preaching and for veterans, we are invited to assess the strength and vitality of our preaching. Catholic preaching finds its authentication in its fidelity to the truth and through the grace of the divine mission that the Church has received in the solemn mandate of Christ to proclaim the saving truth.

As Father Mele points out, Catholic evangelization is an invitation to encounter the Risen Lord in and through the Sacraments and the homily is a privileged moment of the encounter of the Lord in the Word. Reflecting on the homily as a sacred conversation that is shaped by the liturgy in which it is housed and informed by the whole of Scripture, Tradition and

Culture, Father Mele reminds the preacher of the need to be a student of culture. Effective homilies help people to see the presence of God in the course of the ordinary events of their days and to recognize the bridge between the secular and the sacred. The New Evangelization also calls for the homilist to address in what ways the culture needs to be purified by the Good News. In this regard the homilist is forming evangelizers, calling the listener to live fully their baptismal vocation to a priestly, prophetic and kingly way of life.

To highlight the importance of the New Evangelization, our Holy Father has called for a Year of Faith. Each preacher of the Word, all of us who are responsible for homilies, can use this time as a privileged moment of renewing our ministry of proclamation. The call to bring the Word of God with freshness, ardor and awareness of our particular moment is one we can embrace all the more with the guidance that this volume on *The Art of Catholic Preaching and The New Evangelization* offers.

In this Year of Faith, a personal commitment by the preacher to assess the quality of his preaching and with the Lord's help commit to strengthening his skills will prove to be a special grace not only for the preacher but also for God's people. *Sacred Conversations: The Art of Catholic Preaching and The New Evangelization* is a most welcome contribution to renewing Catholic homiletics.

—*Cardinal Donald Wuerl*
*Archbishop of Washington*

# Introduction
## Preaching On the Threshold

If you're wondering who were the greatest preachers of the last one hundred years, you probably shouldn't look to the Catholic Church.

That, at least, is what two studies conducted in the late 1990s concluded.

The first study, commissioned by *Preaching* magazine in 1999, asked its readers to identify the ten most effective preachers of the twentieth century. Hundreds of nominations poured in. From there, the magazine's editors narrowed the list down to the top twenty and ranked them accordingly. Not a single Catholic priest appeared on the list.

The second study, undertaken a few years earlier by two Baylor University professors, was a bit broader: It sought to compile a list of the one hundred most effective (and still living) preachers in the English-speaking world. To assemble that list, the research team contacted 333 professors of homiletics and solicited their suggestions. The end result was a list that included ninety-nine Protestant preachers and one Catholic priest, Father Walter Burghardt, SJ.[1]

The studies beg two questions.

First, are those results correct?

That, of course, is a matter of opinion. But given the absence of someone such as Archbishop Fulton J. Sheen from the first list and any number of great Catholic preachers from the second list, it's probably safe to say, "No." The Catholic Church in America certainly has its share of men who understand the power of God's Word and know how to communicate that power in the most effective way possible. The absence of such men from those lists may well say more about the subjects surveyed than the survey's subject.

But what if that's not the case? What if the studies were correct? What if, objectively speaking, the Catholic Church's greatest preachers simply don't measure up to the greatest preachers Protestant or Orthodox communities have produced. Does it matter? Is that actually a problem?

## Falling Short

The answer is no . . . and yes.

On the one hand, it doesn't matter if Catholic priests aren't making anyone's top ten lists. At least, it doesn't matter much. It's humble, holy obscurity priests are supposed to be after, not worldwide renown. And, when you stop to think about it, it almost makes sense that Protestant preachers best Catholic homilists in surveys such as those named above. At the center of a Protestant worship service is always a preacher and his words. At the center of the Mass is Christ and his sacrifice. Bread and wine transformed into Body and Blood, ancient words first uttered by God made Man, rituals rooted in synagogue and temple—that's Catholic Liturgy. A priest's own words, no matter how moving or powerful they might be, will always pale in comparison.

And yet, on another level, it does matter. It is a problem that Catholics aren't showing up in surveys of great preachers because it simply confirms what most of us already know: There is a problem with preaching in the Catholic Church—a serious problem. Preaching is not what it should be. Homilies are not what they should be. Parishioners know it, and priests know it. And we've known it for a long time.

In 1983, a survey by *U.S. Catholic* listed "poor preaching" as one of the top three reasons people left the Church. twelve years later, in a survey of fifteen thousand Catholics, the statement that received the least affirmative response was "The priest makes the Gospel real through homilies that apply to our lives." More recently, in March 2010, the official blog of the Archdiocese of Washington featured a post entitled "What Do You Think of Catholic Preaching?" followed by 119 responses. Three of them were positive.[2]

The story just doesn't seem to change. For more than two generations, Catholic preaching and Catholic homilies have continued to fall short.

And the fruit of that problem is more than evident in the lives of Catholic parishes and parishioners.

You've heard the statistics: Only 23 percent of adult Catholics show up for Mass every Sunday. Another 21 percent make it about once a month. The rest come either at Christmas and Easter (24 percent) or not at all (32 percent). The picture gets even grimmer if we look at post-Vatican II Catholics (those born between 1961 and 1981) and Millennial Catholics (those born after 1981). From those demographics only 15 and 17 percent, respectively, make it to Mass on Sundays.[3]

Equally grim are the statistics that confirm what most of us have long suspected. Catholics are living together outside of marriage, contracepting, divorcing, and embracing political secularism at about the same rate as non-Catholics. In fact, when it comes to cultural hot button issues such as embryonic stem cell research and same-sex marriage, Catholics reject the Church's teachings in *greater* numbers than the rest of the culture.[4]

Those statistics, of course, are just numbers. They give the barest sketch of what's really going on in the hearts and minds of Catholics today. But that sketch still tells us that there is a deep woundedness in the men and women who sit before priests on Sundays. So many, even among the most faithful, are hurting and hurting badly. The culture has lied to them and led them down the wrong path. Many of them know that and want to find the right way, the right path. Others are so wounded that they no longer know if there is a right path. All, however, in one way or another, are struggling. And all have come to the Church, whether they realize it or not, looking for help. They're looking for truth. They're looking for love. They're looking for hope. And far too often, they're not getting that.

As preachers, too many Catholic priests are not doing what they're ordained to do. They're not leading people to a transforming encounter with Christ. They're not leading them deeper into the Christian mystery. And they're not equipping them to teach, witness, and live that mystery in the world.

Why is that? And what can be done about it?

## THE DISMANTLING OF THE REREDOS

In the years before the Second Vatican Council, beautiful reredoses once stood behind the high altars of small parishes and grand cathedrals alike. Ornamental screens of marble, wood, stone, metal, or ivory, reredoses typically contained niches that held the carved statues of angels and saints. Those figures were beautiful, but they weren't merely decorative. They served an almost liturgical function. They reminded the priest and the congregation gathered that as they prayed the Sacred Liturgy, they stood on the threshold of heaven. The words and actions of the Mass brought them into a sacred conversation with God and all the heavenly hosts.

In the wake of the Second Vatican Council, most Catholic reredoses were dismantled. Those who took them down believed they were heeding *Sacrosanctum concilium's* call for a "noble simplicity" in church design.[5] But when the reredoses went, so did a perpetual, visual, incarnational reminder of that sacred conversation between heaven and earth. The Mass was still the Mass. The objective act was still the same. But the subjective experience was different. For countless Catholics, it became a little less rich, a little less full, a little less beautiful. Without the reredos to remind them of where they stood when they prayed—the threshold of heaven—the people saw less clearly the sacredness of the act in which they participated. And their experience of the Mass was all the poorer for that.

The purpose and fate of liturgical preaching is not unlike that of the reredos, except that the homily isn't just a reminder of the sacred conversation taking place between heaven and earth: It's part of that conversation. In the homily, the priest facilitates a prayerful conversation between Christ and his people, explaining the Word of God, applying it, showing its relevance to their lives and times, and inspiring the congregation to live that Word everyday. As the priest does that, he stands on the threshold of heaven, speaking eternal truths to the temporal moment and preparing people for an encounter with Christ in the Eucharist.

At least, that's what the priest is supposed to do.

In the wake of the Second Vatican Council, as the sign of the sacred conversation—the reredoses—were dismantled, the sacred conversation itself suffered a blow. Liturgical preaching became something far less than it was supposed to be—less sacred, less powerful, less effective, less true. Like the dismantling of the reredos, this didn't happen always and everywhere. But it happened more often than not. And the faithfuls' experience of both Catholic liturgy and Catholic life became immeasurably poorer for that.

Unfortunately, there is no easy "why" behind the dismantling of Catholic homiletics. In part, that's because the problems in homiletics can't be separated from the other problems in Catholic life and liturgy that rocked the Church in the wake of the Second Vatican Council. The problems in preaching and the priesthood, the Mass and the culture are all of a piece. They can't be understood apart from one another, and they can't be corrected apart from one another. They can only be corrected together, through a "reform of the reform."

## The "Reform of the Reform"

Long before he became Pope Benedict XVI, Cardinal Joseph Ratzinger spoke about the need for a "reform of the reform."[6] He knew the path the Fathers of Vatican II intended to set the Church upon. He knew the importance and necessity of following that path. And he knew that was not the path many had followed. In the late 1960s, claiming and often believing they were heeding the Council's instructions, bishops and priests, liturgists and theologians set off in a different direction—one that was often disruptive, utilitarian, and pragmatic—taking along with them countless numbers of the Catholic faithful and, unfortunately, losing many of them along the way.

The "reform of the reform" for which Ratzinger has continued to call in his papacy is something akin to a course correction. It's not, in its essence, punitive or remedial, but simply a return to the intended path—a full, dramatic, narrative configuration—laid out for the Church by the Holy Spirit working through the Council Fathers.

The aim of this book is to examine how the "reform of the reform" applies to Catholic homiletics—the art of preaching—and how a fuller, more faithful homiletics can, in turn, contribute to the larger "reform of the reform" of which Benedict speaks.

Its purpose is in no way to question the gift that the Second Vatican Council was to the Church and to the world. Through it, we have received so much that is good and so much that is necessary for carrying out our sacred mission in this culture. But, in the attempted implementation of that good, we've lost a great deal as well.

## Restoration

Recapturing what was lost and rebuilding a Catholic homiletic that is faithful to both Catholic Tradition and the hopes of the Second Vatican Council is rather like the process for restoring a reredos to its rightful place in a church. Before you can rebuild it, you need to do the foundation work, taking steps to ensure that a right and strong substructure is in place. The first of those steps is to ask how and why the original structure was dismantled. The second step is to consider the site where you will place the reredos: What is its context in space and time? Once those steps have been taken, you lay the actual foundation, putting a solid surface in place on which you can build. Then you build. That phase, the construction phase, is conducted according to a well-drawn out design and carried out by the best craftsmen using the proper tools and building according to time-tested methods. The result of that process is, inevitably, a thing of beauty and a thing that lasts.

When it comes to rebuilding and renewing Catholic homiletics, we do the same, starting with the foundation work. First we look to what the Fathers of Vatican II set out to accomplish, how those accomplishments were undermined, and how that impacted preaching. Then we consider for whom and in what setting priests preach, seeking to understand the struggles, hopes, and needs of the culture and the Catholic congregation. Next comes the actual foundation. We establish a clear vision of the structure upon which Catholic homiletics rests, the Sacred Liturgy, examining what the liturgy is and how the homily fits into that design.

Once the foundation is in place, we move on to the construction phase. That stage of the process begins by outlining the design of a homiletics that takes into account the hopes and objectives of the Second Vatican Council, the struggles and needs of Catholics today, and the liturgical context in which homilies are preached. Then, we look at what it takes to implement those designs: the priest (his character and his understanding of the task at hand) and the tools he wields (the nuts and bolts of homily preparation and delivery).

Through that process, I believe it is possible to piece back together all the fragments that form the context and content of Catholic liturgical preaching, giving rise to a new kind of homiletics, a homiletics that is faithful to the past, relevant to the present, and fruitful in the future. The end result may not mean more priests on anyone's top ten lists, but that's never been the Church's goal. Her goal is to enable priests to preach the words people need to hear, words that enable people to "have life, and have it abundantly," and words that ultimately lead to an encounter with the Author of Life himself (Jn. 10:10).

# Part I

Laying the Foundation

# 1

## The Historical Foundation:
## Conciliar Hopes and Post-Conciliar Confusion

Before we can rebuild Catholic homiletics we need to lay a solid foundation for renewal. The first step in laying that foundation is understanding the Second Vatican Council, as well as all that followed on its heels. And for me, understanding the Second Vatican Council begins with football.

Let me explain.

As a kid growing up in Pittsburgh, I loved football, especially high school football. I loved the game. I loved the crowds. I loved everything about it. But when I entered seminary I was told I had to give that love up. And I had to do it in a very tangible way.

In Cincinnati, Ohio, where I went to seminary, one of the local Catholic high schools was situated right next to the minor seminary. As it so happened, my bedroom looked out on the football field. On Friday nights, the parking lot would fill with students, parents, and alumni. Through the window, I could hear the crowds, hear the band, and hear the referees' whistles. But I couldn't *see* any of it. All the seminarians on that side of the building were ordered to keep our blinds down on Friday nights. We had to shut out the games as part of our priestly formation. It was a way of training us to shut out the world. Needless to say, that training felt like torture.

But I hung in there, and eight years later was ordained a priest. I've never forgotten though how wrong and unnatural it felt, sitting at my desk on a Friday night, hearing the crowds cheer and not being able to be a part of that. More than almost anything else, that experience helped me understand what Vatican II was after. It wanted the Church to raise the blinds and open the windows, to remove the unnatural divisions between

Church and culture so that Christ's redeeming work could be applied to the modern world. That was, they believed, the only way to save the culture. It was also the only way for the Church to be who she was called to be.

Pope John XXIII, however, didn't call the Second Vatican Council to change the Church. He called it to change the world.

## The Hopes of Vatican II

By 1958, the fruits of modernism were in full flower in the West. Some of those fruits were good, i.e. better standards of living, education, and healthcare; others, less so. Rationalism, atheism, and a radical individualism were on the rise, as was the widespread questioning of traditional teachings on faith and morals. The havoc wrought by two world wars, the Holocaust, and the implications of Hiroshima and Nagasaki had made the old answers to those questions sound inadequate, almost trite. And the needs of people living outside Western culture, in the world's developing nations, were coming into the foreground.

The world had changed. The Church had not. And communication between the two was growing more difficult by the day. It also was growing more imperative. More than ever, the world needed to hear what the Church had to say. It needed the truth and grace and life that only the Church could give. The Church didn't need to change its message in order to make that happen, but it did need to change how it communicated that message. It needed to find new ways of saying the same old things so that it could reach people, touch people, and transform people. It also needed to better understand the questions and objections getting in the way of genuine conversion—questions and objections resulting from modernity, the wars, and the philosophical madness wrought by both.

So John XXIII called a council. It opened on October 11, 1962. In his opening address, he laid out his overarching hope for the proceedings: "The greatest concern of the Ecumenical Council is this: that the Sacred Deposit of Christian doctrine should be guarded and taught more efficaciously. That doctrine embraces the whole of man, composed as he is of body and soul. And since he is a pilgrim on this earth, it commands him to tend always toward Heaven."[1]

## THE FIVE PILLARS OF VATICAN II

The framework that the Council Fathers believed would help them achieve their desired end can be summed up in five words: *aggiornamento, ressourcement,* holiness, dialogue, and ecumenical. Those are the pillars upon which the hopes of Vatican II were built.

### Aggiornamento

> Illuminated by the light of this Council, the Church—we confidently trust—will become greater in spiritual riches and gaining the strength of new energies therefrom, she will look to the future without fear. In fact, by bringing herself up to date where required, and by the wise organization of mutual co-operation, the Church will make men, families, and peoples really turn their minds to heavenly things.
> —*Pope John XXIII, Opening Address to the Second Vatican Council, October 11, 1962*

"Fresh beginning"—that's the meaning the Italian word *aggiornamento* conveys. Like the phrase *la dolce vita*, it speaks of a desire to breathe in fresh, invigorating air, to throw open a window and take in all the day has to offer.

For Pope John XXIII, the idea of applying the term to the Church came from Bishop Radini Tedeschi, under whom he served in the Diocese of Bergamo. The bishop, a fiery, disciplined, and energetic administrator, believed that the best way to govern a diocese was not so much to carry out reforms, but rather to maintain the traditions of a diocese while interpreting them in harmony with the new conditions and needs of the time. The pope expressed his aims in the same language: the revivifying of tradition through a renewed relationship with the outside world.[2]

By throwing open a window to the culture, John XXIII believed all that had grown stilted or stale in the Church could be reinvigorated. What was good in the culture, what was fresh, vibrant, and effective, could be used to reframe the Church's engagement with her own and with the world. Similarly, with that window open, the Church herself could reach out more effectively to the world, giving the men and women living in it the life that only the Church could give.

## Ressourcement

> Through the reading and study of the sacred books "the word of God may spread rapidly and be glorified" (2 Thess. 3:1) and the treasure of revelation, entrusted to the Church, may more and more fill the hearts of men. Just as the life of the Church is strengthened through more frequent celebration of the Eucharistic mystery, similarly we may hope for a new stimulus for the life of the Spirit from a growing reverence for the word of God, which "lasts forever" (Is. 40:8; see 1 Peter 1:23–25).
>
> —*Dei Verbum, no. 26*

The decades leading up to the Council were marked not only by rapidly encroaching modernism and secularism, but also by a fervor of activity among some of the Church's most faithful and intelligent scholars: Romano Guardini, Karl Adam, Henri DeLubac, Jean Danielou, Yves Congar, Louis Boyer, Hans Urs von Balthasar, and many more. Their activity was ultimately a response to the expansion of secularism and the crisis it was creating in the Church. They wanted to find more effective ways to speak to the contemporary world, and concluded that in order to do that the Church needed to recover her history. To describe that recovery, they used the term *ressourcement*.

*Ressourcement*, they believed, was a necessary precursor to *aggiornamento*. The renewal of the Church had to begin with a rediscovery of the riches of the whole of her tradition. But by that, they didn't mean a more historically accurate understanding of the Christian past. Rather, what they sought, in the words of Congar, was "a recentering in the person of Christ and his paschal mystery."[3]

In essence, the *nouvelle* theologians wanted the Church to dive back into the headwaters of the Christian faith, recovering a sense of the Christian mystery and God's transcendence, a sense of which many felt neo-scholasticism had unwittingly stripped the faith and which needed to be recovered before the Church could speak to a world fast losing its faith. That sense, they believed could be found in the writings of the Church Fathers and, above all, in the pages of Sacred Scripture. Accordingly, to those pages and to Christ himself the Fathers of Vatican II sought to turn the Church's gaze.

## Holiness

> Thus it is evident to everyone, that all the faithful of Christ of whatever rank or status, are called to the fullness of the Christian life and to the perfection of charity; by this holiness as such a more human manner of living is promoted in this earthly society.
>
> —*Lumen gentium, no. 40*

Church good. World bad. If you're looking for a quick summation of the popular understanding of the universe held by some Catholics in the years leading up to the Council, that ought to do it. It was almost as if the world had a contagious disease and the only way to protect oneself from it was to shut one's self up inside the Church. Because of that, an almost equal number of Catholics held the laity to a different standard than priests and religious. They expected the laity to be good Catholics—pious, devout, and generous, avoiding sin and striving for virtue—but, in general, sainthood was considered a bit above their pay grade. It was, in fact, believed to be the special province of the ordained and consecrated.

The Second Vatican Council set out to turn that idea on its head. The Council Fathers recognized that the double standard, always insidious, was becoming exponentially so in the modern world. Catholic culture was crumbling, traditional societal supports were weakening, and the bar for what it meant to be a "good Catholic" was inching lower and lower. To counteract that, the Church needed saints—saints in the marketplace and home, as well as in the rectories and convents. It needed to reiterate what the Church had, in truth, always known—that God calls everyone, not just priests and religious, to sanctity. Glory, not purgatory, is what all should aim for.

## Dialogue

> The world does not seem prepared to listen to us. But the fact is we are not prepared to talk to it.
>
> —*Cardinal Suens, Fourth Session of the*
> *Vatican Council, October 7, 1965*[4]

John XXIII knew when he called the Council that the world desperately needed to hear what the Church had to say. But before Catholics could engage the culture in a dialog, it first needed to engage *itself* in a dialog about Church teaching, the complex challenges facing modern society, and how the former could illuminate the latter.

This dialog was necessary because then, like today, Catholics tended to isolate themselves into ideological ghettos. Self-identified "conservative" Catholics and self-identified "liberal" Catholics read their own publications, listened to their own speakers, and affiliated primarily with people who shared their worldview. Vatican II wanted to get Catholics of varying viewpoints talking to one another again.

The Fathers understood that Catholics couldn't help anyone unless they recovered a shared spiritual framework and acquired a real and deep understanding of what ailed the world. True self-awareness and true cultural awareness were prerequisites to Catholics reaching out to the larger society. So too was a shared language, a clear grasp of how to speak to the problems in the culture.

## Ecumenical

> The joys and the hopes, the griefs and the anxieties of
> the men of this age, especially those who are poor or in
> any way afflicted, these are the joys and hopes, the griefs

and anxieties of the followers of Christ. Indeed, nothing genuinely human fails to raise an echo in their hearts.

—*Gaudium et spes, no.1*

It wasn't, of course, just a dialog within the Church that the Council sought. It also wanted to spark a dialog between the Church and the world. And by the world, they meant the whole world—with believers and non-believers, rich and poor, those from the North and South, East and West. But in order to do that, the whole Church needed to participate in that conversation. And that could happen only one way: through an ecumenical council.

In the history of the Catholic Church, there have been twenty-one ecumenical councils. They've been held in Asia Minor, Italy, France, and Germany and lasted anywhere from a few months to eighteen years. Summing up the work of the various councils, Catholic theologian and historian George Weigel writes: "Ecumenical councils have defined dogma, written creeds, condemned heresy, laid down guidelines for sacramental practice, deposed emperors, fought schisms, and proposed schemes for the reunification of Christianity."[5] They've been a rather important force for shaping Catholic life and teaching. To call for one, let alone hold one, is no small thing.

John XXIII knew that and was just as surprised as everyone else by the idea of an ecumenical council. In his opening address, the pope described the moment where the idea came to him: "It was completely unexpected," he told the gathered bishops. "It was like a flash of heavenly light, shedding sweetness in eyes and hearts."[6]

That flash, when realized, guaranteed, that the "whole Church" was present at the Council. The Church is, of course, much more than just her bishops. She is also her priests, her religious, and her laity, the entire people of God, Suffering, Militant, and Triumphant. But no conference room on earth could ever hold the Church entire. What one could hold were all the world's bishops, the individual presence of each guaranteeing the presence of the individual local churches. And that presence, universal in scope, guaranteed that the Church could indeed dialogue with the whole world.

## FRUSTRATED HOPES: A TWIST IN TIME

Vatican II sought renewal. It sought a deeper immersion in the past in order to drink more deeply from the source of the Catholic faith, the person Jesus Christ. It also sought to inspire all Christians to pursue holiness, to bring Catholics into a dialog with one another, and to make possible a dialog with the whole of the world.

It articulated those hopes in four sessions spanning three years. And from the wide-ranging conversations that took place amongst the bishops and those observing the Council to the conciliar documents the Council Fathers produced, the aims of *aggiornamento* and *ressourcement*, the call for holiness and dialogue, and the ecumenical nature of the conference established the framework for the Church's work in the coming millennium.

In the first years and even decades after the Council, however, it was difficult for many within the Church to believe that the fruits of renewal would ever come. Rather than pointing the Church in the right direction, its five organizing principles were, almost more often than not, misinterpreted and misapplied, causing untold problems in the Church's life, liturgy, and, of course, liturgical preaching.[7]

### Remaking vs. Renewing

Almost from the start, the Church's call for *aggiornamento* was misunderstood. Rather than interpreting it as a call for a renewal of the Church's traditions, many took the word to mean, more simply, "change." It was linked to the idea of a post-Tridentine Church, a Church that would be remade in line with modernity.

Those primarily responsible for that linking were American and European clergy who had been advocating for change for some time. They wanted a more "current" Church, one more in accord with the thinking of cultural elites. Even before the Council, theologians such as Louis Boyer and Henri de Lubac warned that certain programs of "adaptation" were afoot, "which, having cut all moorings to tradition, were rapidly drifting towards servile adaptation to the world and to its changing idols."[8]

That "adaptation" shifted into high-gear after the Council, when *aggiornamento* became the excuse for any number of problematic agendas and innovations, from priests giving the okay to their parishioners using contraception to religious discarding their habits. The Church's biblical theologians, who had been wandering slowly off the reservation ever since *Divino Afflante Spiritu* was published in 1943, broke into an all-out run, sprinting to catch up with their Marxist and feminist peers and centuries of dubious biblical criticism. Many systematic theologians did likewise, declaring their independence from the Magisterium alongside Catholic colleges and universities, the latter going so far as to sign their own "Declaration of Independence" in 1967 at the Land 'O Lakes Conference.

In the liturgy, a misunderstanding of *aggiornamento* led to the almost total abandonment of Latin, as well as the abandonment of older musical forms and hymns in favor of "parish tea party liturgies" and contemporary musical norms. Traditional Catholic practices, such as 40 Hours Devotions, meatless Fridays, and May crownings, were similarly forsaken, their simplicity and piety at odds with the modern, sophisticated image some Catholics wanted the Church to cultivate.

Those problems carried over into the realm of preaching, where, rather than critiquing modernity and its problems and allowing that understanding to both shape the way they articulated the ancient truths of the faith and applied them to contemporary life, many priests began allowing modernity to instead shape their understanding of Church teaching. They saw the faith through the lens of the world, rather than the world through the lens of faith.

At times, that meant the faith wasn't preached in all its fullness: The more difficult subject matters—consumerism, hedonism, narcissism, conformism—were simply not discussed from the pulpit. Instead, the Gospel message and the demands it places on believers was boiled down to a non-controversial, "Jesus was a nice guy, so you should be nice too." At other times, Catholic teaching was denied outright. Priests rationalized miracles, such as the feeding of the five thousand in Matthew 14, (it became the "miracle of sharing"), while others used their homilies to oppose *Humanae vitae* and Apostolic Tradition.

The direction of Catholic Scripture scholarship complicated matters even further. Seminary and university professors often spent more time in the classroom discussing various theories of biblical authorship than they did teaching seminarians how to use Scripture to preach. Seminarians were likewise schooled in the supposed errors of Scripture, which meant that their faith in God's Word was often weakened, rather than strengthened, by their studies. Many began their priestly ministry feeling unequipped to read, understand, or preach Sacred Scripture. Many others began with no reservations about using the homily as a forum for critiquing, undermining, or twisting the biblical readings to their own desired ends.

Lastly, in the early days after the Council, an incorrect understanding of *aggiornamento* was the direct cause of countless homiletical innovations that flew in the face of the sacred nature of the Mass. From starting the homily off with a cartwheel (to get the congregation's attention) to wearing clown noses and bringing donkeys and ducks into the sanctuary, "creativity" was the order of the day. Priests young and old (myself included) thought it our duty to shake things up, to use our preaching to let in that much talked about fresh air. More often than not, however, all we let in were a series of distractions, which pulled people's attention away from the supernatural mysteries unfolding before their eyes. When that happened, the homily became about us and what we had to offer. Christ and what he had to offer got lost in the shuffle.

## Pre-Conciliar vs. Post-Conciliar

Like *aggiornamento*, the misinterpretation of *ressourcement* began almost before the Council ended. The word quickly came to be understood not only as a recovery of earlier traditions, with their emphasis on a mysterious, transcendent, and personal God, but also as a rejection of anything "medieval" or "Tridentine." In Catholic high schools, universities, and seminaries, this often meant that the clear, sound, philosophical reasoning of Thomas and the scholastics wasn't supplemented and counter-balanced with the richness of the Fathers and Scripture: It was thrown out wholesale, leaving a glaring gap in Catholics' philosophical and theological formation. A similar phenomenon occurred in parishes, where statuary, stained glass, and altar rails were tossed out faster than Thomism was from the universities.

This modern "stripping of the altars" originated in a rightly ordered desire to reintroduce simplicity into church design and décor, eliminating some of the excess and mawkishness that had worked its way into parishes during the late nineteenth and early twentieth centuries. But in the process, reformers often made the mistake of "throwing the baby out with the bathwater," rejecting theologically sound and aesthetically pleasing architectural principles, as well as the importance of devotional art work. The cold and barren result fell far short of noble simplicity, with both the remodeled and newly built churches proclaiming more the centrality of man than communion with God.

On the liturgical end of the spectrum, set liturgical rites became viewed in many quarters as stuffy, uncreative, and stifling to the "Spirit." Devotional practices, from the Rosary to Eucharistic processions and Benediction were likewise dismissed as "medieval inventions," inappropriate for a "post-conciliar" Church. The sacraments received a similar treatment. The Eucharist's sacrificial nature was downplayed, and viewed increasingly as a "meal," with alternative matter (sour dough bread, honey and raisin loaves, even tortilla chips) "substituted" for unleavened bread. In some dioceses, children began making their First Communion years before their First Confession, while elsewhere, priests made common use of communal absolution and told parishioners that the confessional had gone the way of the '62 missal.

What did seem to go the way of the '62 missal, at least in many parishes, was the inclusion of catechesis in homilies. *Ressourcement* rightly demanded a greater focus on putting the Scriptures and Tradition into a dialog with contemporary life. But some priests saw that demand and catechetical formation as two mutually exclusive tasks. To them, breaking open the Word signaled a complete break from catechetical homilies, which had been the norm before Vatican II. Bernard Cooke described how, in the years preceding the Council, priests were expected to preach in such a way as "to feed the people with salutary words, teaching them what they must know for salvation, telling them clearly and briefly what vices they should avoid and what virtues they should acquire in order to avoid eternal punishment and gain heavenly glory."[9]

As desirable as that might seem to some Catholics, weary of the "Jesus was nice, so you be nice too" variety of homilies, there were problems with that formula—most notably the over-simplified approach to the human struggle with sin and virtue and a failure to use the Scriptures to speak to the culture. But despite those problems, there was and is something to be said for including at least some catechesis and spiritual formation in homilies. For many Catholics, the Sunday homily is the only place they're going to get any of either, and its widespread abandonment within the homily bears at least part of the responsibility for the theological illiteracy that spread rapidly among Catholics in the post-Vatican II era.

## God vs. Us

Catholics' initial understanding and pursuit of the universal call to holiness fared little better than their efforts at *aggiornamento* and *ressourcement*. The call, so powerfully stated in *Lumen gentium* and restated in 1965's *Apostolicam actuositatem*, was, by many, ignored. By others it was confused with Catholics' obligation to work for social justice. And with the need for an interior transformation and growth in the cardinal virtues so often disregarded, championing the rights of minorities and the poor became, *de facto*, the defining hallmarks of Catholics' role in the world.

That misunderstanding of holiness blurred the line between the ministerial priesthood and the universal priesthood of the laity. That blurring, in a great many cases, led people to understand the call for the full and active participation of the people in the liturgy not as the interior participation intended by the Council Fathers—a spiritual immersion in the mysteries of the Holy Mass—but rather as a participation defined by liturgical function. Roles for the laity within the liturgy multiplied, and the sacred nature and unique importance of the ordained minister was diminished. Priests sat out on the distribution of Communion in order to allow more laity to function as extraordinary ministers of Holy Communion. Other priests invited the congregation to pray the prayers reserved for the priest or to gather around the altar as de-facto concelebrants.

The emphasis on the dignity of the laity's call also unwittingly contributed to a neglect of the proper humility men are called to show in the presence of God. Kneeling in many quarters was abandoned, with newer parishes all too often constructed without any kneelers at all. Other parishes were constructed in the round, with the tabernacle placed far from sight and crucifixes removed, making the priest and the congregation gathered, not Christ, the visual focal point during worship. Liturgical music likewise began celebrating the community (as opposed to Christ), featuring lyrics such as those from Tom Conry's "Anthem" ("We are called. We are chosen . . . We are sign. We are wonder . . . We are question. We are creed.").

That understanding of the liturgy, an understanding that failed to fully grasp that the Mass is a transcendent encounter with Christ, a participation in the sacrifice of Good Friday and the joy of Easter Sunday, allowed a one-sided understanding of the universal call to holiness to work its way into the homily as well. It was social action, more than repentance, conversion, and evangelization, that was encouraged. And it was corporal works of mercy, not the inner transformation that makes good works bear good fruit, that was more often stressed. As such, the priest wasn't directing the congregation's gaze to the altar and the Eucharistic Christ, but rather to themselves and to the world. The heart of the homily and one of the most important things that sets it apart from ordinary preaching—its orientation to an imminent encounter with Christ—was all too often missing.

### Dialogue vs. Self-Absorption

On the dialogue front, the intra-Catholic conversation so hoped for by the Council ended up focusing more on internal politics and liturgy than on theology and philosophy. At first, that was somewhat understandable. What functions the laity could and could not assume in the Mass, the introduction of the vernacular in worship, and how long religious habits really needed to be were immediate questions that concretely impacted the lives of those asking them. In some ways, it was only natural that they received the most attention in the years first following the Council.

But in many places the conversation never moved on. In fact, it spiraled downward until discussions over the color of the rectory's carpet took up more time than discussions about how to better evangelize the community. Meanwhile, the questions with which the Council Fathers wanted Catholics to grapple—questions such as the impact of media on communities, the importance of marriage and family to a civil society, the responsibility of individuals to one another in a just state—went undiscussed.

Within the liturgy, the homily was ground central for this stunted dialogue. As with *aggiornamento*, it was frequently the culture, not the Church, doing the talking in the priest's homily, with a secular perspective shaping the ideas discussed. Rather than using the Scriptures and Catholic Tradition to give Catholics a theological and philosophical framework that could help them make sense of the issues with which they were wrestling— divorce, contraception, cohabitation, abortion, finances, consumerism, civil rights, the feminist movement, etc.—many priests remained silent. They failed to give Catholics the lens they needed to make sense of the contemporary world and engage it with Christian truth. Instead, they left them with the difficult task of forming their consciences alone, without the Church's help.

## Ecumenical vs. Syncretism

Finally, the ecumenical nature of the Council, a nature intended to reflect the Church's concern, respect, and responsibility for all the world's people, became confused with a wrong-headed understanding of ecumenism.

Strictly speaking, ecumenism has as its goal nothing less than "the full communion of Christians in one apostolic faith and in one eucharistic fellowship at the service of a truly common witness." That communion, in turn, is intended to both reflect the communion of the Father, Son, and Holy Spirit, and fulfill Christ's prayer at the Last Supper, "that they all may be one" (Jn. 17:21).[10]

From the start, John XXIII made it clear that the Roman Catholic Church was fully committed to that kind of ecumenism. The Council's verbal recognition that the body of Christ "subsists" in the Roman Catholic Church, but that "many elements of sanctification and of truth are found outside its visible confines," reflected that commitment. So too did its statements that all baptized believers "have a right to be called Christians and accepted as brothers by the children of the Church," and that "the Catholic Church rejects nothing of what is true and holy in [non-Christian] religions."[11]

Statements like that told Catholics that relations with those outside the visible Church needed to be grounded in respect. They highlighted the Church's proper concern for all God's children and called Catholic priests, religious, and laity to act upon that concern. In that, they reflected the ecumenical nature of the Council. They were never intended, however, to suggest anything contrary to that which the Church has always believed about herself, namely that Christ established the Catholic Church to be his Body and Bride and that the fullness of truth can be found only within her.

Rather than recognizing that, however, some Catholics understood the Council's statements as an endorsement of the broadest kind of ecumenism, an ecumenism almost akin to syncretism. In other words, they interpreted the Council's words as a declaration that the Catholic faith was no better or truer than any other faith. They also inferred from that conclusion that, like all other religions, it was, in some ways, wrong. They inferred that the deposit of faith contained errors. In effect, they turned the Council's acknowledgement that other religions contained shards of truth inside out, failing to recognize that those shards of truth were truths already possessed in full by the Catholic Church.

The results, not surprisingly, were disastrous for evangelization. Far too many Catholics, ordained and non-ordained, came to believe that there was no imperative to share the faith or explain it. In Catholic universities, theology departments were supplanted by "religious studies" departments, with the Catholic faith routinely receiving little or no pride of place. Elsewhere, religious sisters and priests took to mining other faiths for spiritual wisdom, often abandoning their own traditions in the process. Occasionally, those foreign spiritual practices were imported into the Mass and parish life, with religious communities participating in "Buddhist-Catholic" liturgies, priests chanting Sanskrit peace mantras at the consecration, and parishes offering workshops on centering prayer.

The inclusion of readings from the Tibetan Book of Life within the homily or priests expounding on what the neo-Gnostics thought of Mary Magdalene confused matters even more. Homilies lost their evangelistic bent as well as their catechetical bent. God's redeeming action in salvation history, a history chronicled in the pages of Sacred Scripture and actualized in the Holy Mass, became not an actual fact, a reality playing out before the congregation's eyes and one in which they were called to participate, but rather just another story describing the heart of man's plight on earth. It became just another version of the Buddhist, Hindu, and rabbinical myths that their priests used to explain the Sunday Gospel. The nature of truth itself, in all its absoluteness, was diminished in the very place where it was supposed to be proclaimed.

༈

The Second Vatican Council came to an end nearly fifty years ago, and in the dioceses, parishes, schools, and apostolates where the hopes and goals of the Council Fathers were implemented fully and faithfully, the five organizing principles of Vatican II became powerful sources of renewal in the Church. Just as the Fathers intended, they now guide how many Catholics in those locals live, worship, and believe. But even in those places, renewal was a long time coming. And in far too many other places, it has yet to arrive.

Most of the initial silliness—Sanskrit peace mantras, dancing priests, and cartwheels in the sanctuary—has ceased. But vestiges remain. And more than vestiges remain of the poor formation priests, religious, and laity received courtesy of the worst post-Vatican II errors. There are Catholics of all ages, states in life, and vocations who still subscribe to the twisted understanding of the Council's primary aims. That shows up in the way they worship and the way they live. It also shows up in the way priests preach.

Today, you would be hard-pressed to find a priest trying to consecrate a bowl of Doritos, but walk into many a parish on a Sunday and you'll find the misinterpretations of *aggiornamento, ressourcement,* holiness, dialogue, and ecumenical still incarnating themselves in the priest's homily. There, the early errors linger. Priests may not be quoting *The Prophet* in their homilies, but weak homilies—homilies that do not teach, do not engage, do not challenge, and do not lead people to an encounter with the Eucharistic Christ—are far too common. There are some exceptionally fine Catholic homilists out there, far more than get credit for the good work they do. But most others are adequate at best.

This is exactly why this tour through the history of Vatican II and its aftermath was necessary. It helps answer the question on so many Catholic minds: Why can't priests preach? It also prepares the way for answering the question on the minds of so many bishops, seminary rectors, and homiletics professors: "What will it take to form priests who can preach to the Church today?"

# 2

## The Human Foundation:
## Seeing the Culture and the Congregation Rightly

They say all politics is local. In a way, the same can be said of preaching. All preaching is local. It happens in a specific time and place, not a vacuum. And each parish, hospital chapel, or Newman Center where a priest offers the Mass has its own ever-changing set of human dynamics.

Some congregations are poor. Others wealthy. Some congregations are situated in the middle of inner city war zones. Others perched in the hinterlands of suburbia. There are parishes that have been steeped in orthodoxy and orthopraxis for years. And there are parishes reeling from scandal, incorrect teaching, and financial mismanagement.

The same holds true for the parishioners sitting in the pews. Almost every time they preach, priests have the daunting task of delivering a homily to a congregation composed of eighty-six-year-old widows and sixteen-year-old boys. There are young mothers in the pews doing battle with their brood, and there are agitated bachelors sitting right behind them, glaring at those mothers as they do battle with their brood.

Every time a priest delivers a homily, he delivers it in the midst of a veritable mishmash of the human condition. He speaks not to people in general, but to people in particular, people with names, faces, and stories. And, in order to craft a homily that speaks to each and every person looking up at him, he needs, as much as possible, to know their names, faces, and stories. He needs to have a relationship with the people to whom he preaches. The closer a priest is to his congregation—the more aware he is of what's going on in their daily lives—the more he can speak to them in the homily as a father and friend.

A full, faithful, and effective Catholic homiletics, however, requires more than just knowing who's sending their oldest off to college and who's eating dinner alone. It means knowing the cultural forces shaping the superstructure of people's lives.

## The American Meta-Culture

For all the differences that exist between communities and parishioners, they all still have one thing in common. They call twenty-first century America home. It doesn't matter if parishioners are black or white, rich or poor, six or sixty-six. Their ancestors may have come over on the Mayflower, or they themselves might have snuck across the border last week. They might be in church every morning at 6 am or they might only darken the parish door at Christmas and Easter. Regardless, if they are living in this culture right now, they are all being shaped by certain cultural assumptions, temptations, and problems.

It's possible they're succumbing to those assumptions and temptations. It's possible they're rejecting them. It's possible they're caught somewhere in between. Regardless, they can't escape them. They live in the midst of them. And they need their priest to be right there with them, knowing the assumptions, temptations, and problems that surround them and speaking the truths that can guide them safely through the cultural minefield.

This is what *Presbyterorum Ordinis*, the Second Vatican Council's document on the life and ministry of priests, tells us. The document states that priests "cannot be ministers of Christ unless they be witnesses and dispensers of a life other than earthly life."

"But," the document continues, "they cannot be of service to men if they remain strangers to the life and conditions of men" (3).

That's why every priest needs to be a student of the culture. He needs to understand thoroughly the cultural dynamics at work in society today so that he can serve his congregation, helping them navigate through the opportunities and threats the world presents.

On a global level, the Second Vatican Council aimed to do just that. Pope John XXIII wanted the Church to reflect deeply on the modern world and its place in it so that she could find the right ways and words to speak with the world. Only through knowledge and understanding, he believed, could a true conversation between God and his people take place.

In the years leading up to the Council, the tendency of some within the hierarchical Church to isolate themselves from the culture or reject it outright inhibited that conversation. A false dichotomy was frequently set up between the Church and the world, and rather than engage the world, using the good in the culture as springboard for challenging what was problematic, the culture was simply condemned. The good was neither seen nor used.

After the Council, the opposite mistake was even more frequently made. Rather than becoming students of the culture, some Catholic clergy became disciples of it. They didn't challenge cultural assumptions: They promoted them. They didn't question the culture or engage the culture: They embraced it. They allowed themselves to be shaped by the culture, and their preaching reflected that. The conversation the Council Fathers hoped for wasn't taking place, at least not in many Catholic homilies. Priests were talking, but what they were saying was all too often coming just from them. Christ wasn't able to speak to his people. He had been shut out of the conversation.

The "reform of the reform" as it applies to homiletics requires that we invite Christ back in to the conversation, enabling priests to speak now as Christ spoke in history: with love, with honesty, with clarity, and with wisdom, embracing what is good in the culture and helping people choose to reject what is not good. But for that kind of conversation to take place, the priest must see the culture for what it is and understand how it shapes the men and women who fill his parish every Sunday. Cultural knowledge is part of the foundation from which priests must preach. And that knowledge rests on four basic truths about the congregation gathered.

## A CRISIS OF ATTENTION

An author I know often jokes that she writes for "ADD America."

"I have one sentence to capture their attention," she says. "Just one. If I lose them there, I've lost them for good."

The same can almost be said for priests. At the beginning of their homily, they have but a few short seconds to engage the congregation. And once they have their attention, they have to work to keep it. That is no easy task.

That's not to say that no one is paying attention. It's also not to say that those who aren't paying attention don't want to pay attention. Some are and many do. But for most of the former, attention is a struggle, while for most of the latter it's all but impossible. Decades of weak homilies bear some of the blame. In many places people have grown so accustomed to homilies that don't reach them, teach them, inspire them, or challenge them, that tuning out the priest when he starts to speak has simply become a habit.

But that is only a small part of the problem.

Every day 247 billion emails whizz through cyberspace, with more than 100 of those ending up in the average user's inbox. The emails, of course, compete for our attention with more than 234 million Websites, 126 million blogs, and 23.3 million "tweets," sent via the micro-blogging platform "Twitter." In the virtual world, there are also billions of hours of video available via YouTube, 4 billion photos to view on Flicker, and, of course, Facebook, which currently claims more than 500 million users.[1]

Offline, information finds us through talk radio, news radio, network TV, and 1,000 plus cable channels. Throw in text messages, cell phones, and good old-fashioned print media, and it's easy to see why they call this the "Information Age."

The sheer amount of information is overwhelming. The fragmentation of that information even more so. It comes at us in bits and flashes, with pings and beeps and rings. Hyperlinks, embedded videos, and related stories compete with the main story on every website we visit. Sidebars and scrolling news updates do the same in print and on television. The stories in magazines and newspapers are much shorter than they used to be. They are shorter still online. No website worth its salt has only text anymore. They also feature videos, music, interactive forums, and daily surveys. Likewise, at work and school, people rarely hear anyone deliver just a lecture. Public addresses are now multi-media presentations featuring PowerPoint slides, music, videos, and glossy handouts.

All that information (and the bite-size packages in which we receive it) isn't just leaving us as it found us. Rather it's changing who we are, how we live, and how we think.

In her book, *Distracted: The Erosion of Attention and the Coming Dark Age*, Maggie Jackson writes:

> The way we live is eroding our capacity for deep, sustained, perceptive attention—the building block of intimacy, wisdom and cultural progress . . . The seduction of alternative virtual universes, the addictive allure of multi-tasking people and things, our near religious allegiance to a constant state of motion: these are markers of a land of distraction, in which our old conceptions of space, time, and place have been shattered. This is why we are less and less able to see, hear, and comprehend what's relevant and permanent, why so many of us feel that we can barely keep our heads above water, and our days are marked by perpetual loose ends.[2]

A growing body of scientific evidence bears her conclusions out. Experts, such as the Educational Testing Service, report a declining ability among the young to process information accurately. They're less able to discern a source's point of view, connect disparate pieces of knowledge, and frame a sustained argument. Other studies have demonstrated that the average adult worker is capable of spending a mere eleven minutes working on a project before switching to another and is typically interrupted—by email, a phone call, or their own desire to switch tasks—every three minutes. Both adults and teens typically spend no more than sixty seconds on any given web page, with their attention focused for a maximum of only nine seconds.[3]

In this Information Age, we have become a nation of skimmers and skippers, accustomed to having information delivered to us in bright, shiny, easy-to-open packages. Attentive listening no longer comes naturally to most people, Catholics included, and millions of other voices vie against the Church for the few precious seconds of attentiveness people do have to give. Making a priest's task even harder is the fact that the overwhelming majority of those voices have a very different message to proclaim from that which the Church proclaims, messages that are louder, flashier, and usually more artfully articulated.

When priests step to the pulpit to preach, they can no longer assume they have an attentive congregation before them. They can't assume people are listening. Rather, they should assume just the opposite—that people's minds are racing with concerns about work, school, or the small children sitting next to them. Pressing deadlines, troublesome mother-in-laws, and the Pirates latest loss loom large, as do growling stomachs, aching heads, and tired bodies. Many want to pay attention to the priest's homily. They really do. But for some it takes tremendous effort, and for others, it's all but impossible. Vestments alone will not ensure any priest a captive audience. Today, it takes much, much more than that.

## A CRISIS IN CATECHESIS

When a priest preaches, he can't assume attentiveness in the congregation. He also can't assume knowledge of the Catholic faith or even knowledge of Christ.

In the years leading up to the Council, the Church did an excellent job handing on the "what" of the faith. Catholics knew what we were supposed to do. We knew how to say our prayers, what sins to confess, and what feasts to celebrate. We knew what virtues to strive for and what vices to avoid. But what many of us didn't have was the "why." We didn't understand the reason behind the "what." We didn't have the fullness of the Christian story.

Vatican II saw that and wanted to change it. It wanted Catholics, laity as well as priests and religious, to have a deeper understanding of the "why" behind what the Church believed and did. But after the Council, in the midst of the Church's efforts to give people the "why," unhelpful experimentation often led more to the questioning of the doctrines and practices than it did to the explaining of them. There also was a widespread lack of clarity on the content and method of catechesis, with both varying greatly from parish to parish and diocese to diocese.

In a 2009 interview with *Our Sunday Visitor,* the Most Reverend Richard Malone, Bishop of Portland, Maine and Chairman of the Committee on Evangelization and Catechesis for the USCCB, summed up the catechetical problem of the post-conciliar years as one of fragmentation, explaining that, "Rather than approaching catechesis as the handing on of the symphony of faith, people were picking and choosing what they handed on. Even really central truths were not being taught or were being taught incorrectly."[4]

The past two decades have seen the slow reversal of that trend in many places across the U.S. Spurred on by the 1994 publication of the Catechism of the Catholic Church and the other documents that followed in its wake (the *General Directory of Catechesis,* the *National Directory of Catechesis,* the *United States Catholic Catechism for Adults,* etc.), a fuller, more faithful, and more systematic catechesis is finally starting to take hold in many dioceses. But that trend is not uniform. It also has been a long time coming.

Accordingly, almost as often as not, Catholics today still don't know the "what" or the "why" of their faith. According to a 2007 study by the Center for Applied Research in the Apostolate, the Real Presence is foreign to nearly half of adult Catholics, with 43 percent believing that the bread and wine are only "symbols" of Christ's body and blood. The Sunday Mass obligation, Confession, and basic devotions fare even worse. Only 32 percent of Catholics believe it's important to attend Mass every Sunday; 62 percent believe they can be "a good Catholic" without receiving the Sacrament of Reconciliation; 48 percent never pray the Rosary; and only 14 percent participate in Eucharistic Adoration.[5]

Likewise, most Catholics know that the Church says sex outside of marriage and abortion are wrong, but they think it doesn't matter if they disagree. In fact, 58 percent believe abortion should be legal in all or most cases. Another 27 percent believe it should be legal in some cases. And 58 percent believe homosexuality is an acceptable lifestyle. Near equal numbers failed to give rudimentary definitions of the Trinity or the Incarnation. Unfortunately, that's as true of the eighth graders coming in for Confirmation as it is of the 35-year-old parents bringing their baby in for baptism and the 60-year-old retirees who volunteer on Tuesdays at the parish food pantry. They want the sacraments, and many show up at Mass on most Sundays, but they're not exactly sure why they want or do those things.[6]

## The Who

It's not, however, just the "what" of the faith that many are missing. It's also the "who."

In 1981, the U.S. Bishops could write with some confidence that, "to a greater or lesser degree, it is faith in Jesus Christ that is common to all the members of a community gathered for Eucharist."[7]

Thirty years later, such confidence can't be had. As Bishop Malone explained in that same *Our Sunday Visitor* article, "People come to us for catechesis who really have not been adequately evangelized. They have not yet come to know the Lord."[8]

In other words, priests can no longer assume that everyone sitting in the pews on Sunday knows Christ. Many don't. Many have never encountered him. They don't know they're called to have a personal, loving relationship with him. They don't know what that relationship entails. They likewise have never heard about the universal call to holiness. They have a vague notion about God and religious obligation, but not much else.

Again, the numbers bear this out. A 2007 study by the Pew Forum revealed that 29 percent of Catholics believe God is simply "an impersonal force." Further, 40 percent believe a personal relationship with him is impossible. And 43 percent pray infrequently or never.[9]

Those numbers are dismal and depressing. They're also a grim reminder that Catholic preaching has been less than effective for far too long.

None of this, however, means that real belief and knowledge of the faith are absent from parishes on Sunday mornings. Far from it. There are millions of faithful and knowledgeable Catholic laity in this country. In fact, the laity that does know their faith may perhaps know it more deeply and fully than any group of laity in the history of the Church. After all, they are primarily the ones now charged with teaching it in schools, universities, and parish education programs. They are primarily the ones running apostolates, leading Bible studies, and writing faith formation materials. They are the ones populating master's programs in theology and packing summer conferences around the country. It would not be a stretch to say that the Church in the U.S. is blessed with the most active and well-formed Catholic laity in the world.

But despite the active and important presence of these Catholics, the numbers don't lie. Almost half of all Catholics in America today (and on some questions more than half) either don't know what the Church believes or they themselves don't believe it. The Church has not properly shaped their view of the world and themselves. And where the Church has failed, the culture has stepped in.

## A CRISIS IN CATHOLICS' WORLDVIEW

This brings us to the third cultural truth priests must grasp in order to preach effectively. Because there is so much information in our culture and so many competing voices, and because the Church has failed far too often at evangelizing and catechizing the baptized, priests cannot assume that their congregation sees the world though the lens of the Catholic faith. In fact, they need to assume just the opposite, that modernity and post-modernity color Catholics' vision of the world.

### Modernity and Post-Modernity Defined

Modernity, in essence, is a product of the Enlightenment. A few centuries back, man decided it was time to start celebrating man and his accomplishments. History became viewed through the prism of progress—all of time was marching forward and upward, led by the power of reason from glory to glory. Science and mathematics, with their hard facts and quantifiable data, supplanted literature and the arts as the engines of man's advancement. And faith, which couldn't be quantified or judged by the scientific method, became the object of skepticism and derision. God was relegated from foreground to background, and faith and reason—so long intertwined in the West—were split apart.

For a good two hundred years, the vision of the world offered by modernity seemed both plausible and attractive. Man's reason was producing unimaginable wonders—steam ships and horseless carriages, electric lights and flying machines, moving pictures and talking records. Enlightened democracies were coming into being, and slavery was ending. Material goods, from soap to clothing, were suddenly cheaply and readily available. In the midst of all that, humanity can certainly be forgiven for thinking rather well of themselves and believing that if they just worked hard enough, if they were just more reasonable, they might make an Eden of the world once more.

But that rosy vision of progress came to an end in the trenches of Verdun and on the shores of Gallipoli. The mad, mindless slaughter of World War I sewed the seeds of doubt in European minds about history's inevitable march to utopia. Stock market crashes, Hoovervilles, and concentration camps helped spread those seeds Stateside. Vietnam and Watergate fertilized them, and by the time madmen started flying planes into skyscrapers, post-modernism had come into full flower.

Post-modernism is a critique of modernism. It says modernism missed a thing or two in its assessment of the world—that there is more to being human than the capacity to reason, that there is more to knowledge than facts, and that there is more to progress than linear advancement. It also goes beyond that to question the very nature of reason, the very possibility of knowledge, and the very definition of progress. Sometimes it goes further, denying the actual existence of both knowledge and truth.

Unlike modernism, post-modernism believes there is a place for spiritual wisdom. It also tends to prioritize the good of the community over the good of the individual. The problem, however, is that because it denies man's ability to know truth, it also must deny all religious claims to truth. The teachings of Catholicism, like the teachings of Judaism, Hinduism, Buddhism, and Islam, become merely opinions, and "spiritual wisdom" nothing but an ephemeral concept, adaptable to the needs of the individual and held only for as long as it suits. Similarly, with no one faith or philosophy any more or less true than any others, post-modernism denies itself the very means necessary for knowing what the common good is, let alone achieving it.

Describing the results of post-modernism's relativism and nihilism, Father James Wehner writes:

> In practical terms, this is why the New Age movement, with its vague spirituality and loose morality, is booming. This is also why people clamor to build "green" homes or buy T-shirts from the Gap that benefit AIDS victims in Africa, but can't bring themselves to remain faithful in a relationship. Post-modernism is all about easy spirituality, easy morality, and easy counter-cultural living. It's cool to "be spiritual," to help others, and to recycle. It's not cool to say everyone else has to share the same spiritual beliefs, to check our sexual desires, or to embrace real poverty.[10]

That is another way of saying that in the end, post-modernism is a philosophy that produces questions, not answers. It identifies problems, not solutions. It tears down, but never builds up.

## Modernity and Post-Modernity Lived

Because of that, modernism never completely loosened its hold on Western culture in general or American culture in particular. Today, modernism and post-modernism stand side by side, each moving and shaping the culture and the people within it in strange and often contradictory directions.

For example, despite post-modernism's critique of reason and its endorsement of other ways of knowing—spirituality, intuition, emotion—the culture still primarily views reason and faith as competitors, not co-workers, with more heed paid to knowledge that is quantifiable and fact-filled.

Likewise, despite post-modernism's rejection of man-guided progress, man remains at the center of the world. A higher power gets a nod from some on Sundays, from a few more at Christmas and Easter, from most people during weddings and funerals or when natural disasters and jihadi terrorists strike. But the modern/post-modern world remains man's, not God's.

One of the most dangerous consequences of that is a wrong-headed notion of freedom. People believe freedom consists of being free from outside restrictions—free from anyone else telling them what to do—not in being free for something—free for love, free for service, free for virtue. As such, obedience is no longer considered a virtue to cultivate but a mental hang-up to be overcome. Authority is seen as suspect—at best, well-intentioned but incompetent; at worst, evil, oppressive, and corrupt—and the individual is enshrined as the sole arbiter of truth.

Equally problematic is that happiness, joy, and fulfillment are primarily conceived of in material and earthly terms. Most people's understanding of the "good life" matches up with Hollywood and Madison Avenue's idea of the good life, with success measured in dollars, happiness in gadgets, and fulfillment in the number, kind, and variety of sexual encounters. And when those things are had but happiness isn't, people can't understand what went wrong. All too often, the response is simply to pursue those false goods with even more vigor—emptiness leading to excess, and excess leading to even greater emptiness.

The idea that happiness lies in self-denial not self-fulfillment, that joy comes through the acceptance of suffering not the pursuit of pleasure, and that love is about sacrifice not sex simply doesn't occur to hundreds of millions of Americans. They live in a fragmented world, constructed with half-understood truths and self-selected moral codes. They have no vision of the whole, no understanding of a reality larger than themselves. They're looking for meaning, searching for identity, for an understanding of who they are and what they need to be happy, but they have only themselves for guides in that search. And the result of that, inevitably, is despair.

That's how much of the culture thinks. It's also how a good many Catholics think. It shapes the thoughts of some, colors the thoughts of virtually all. Even those who have rejected the worst of modernism and post-modernism still have to contend with it. They have to fight constant temptations to rationalism, skepticism, materialism, and consumerism. They have to work to believe in a God who might ask them to suffer and sacrifice. They have to struggle against the wounds inflicted upon them and those they love by sexual license, pornography, and a sex-saturated culture. And they have to live in a world where nothing seems sacred, solid, or lasting. They also have to worry about speaking out against relativism and secularism, about being considered different, marginalized, or worse, dubbed "intolerant." Pope Benedict has called this the "dictatorship of opinion," and it's a dictatorship that affects both clergy and laity, bidding us to keep silent when silent is the last thing we should be.

## A CRISIS IN THE HUMAN HEART

And that brings us to the last cultural truth priests need to understand in order to understand their congregation and preach effectively.

Not only is it wrong for priests to keep silent on the issues about which we most need to speak—issues of good and evil, faith and morals, truth and lies—but, more importantly, people don't want priests to keep silent. They want priests to speak out. They want to hear the truth preached in all its fullness.

On the surface, it may not seem that way. Priests who speak out against divorce or contraception on Sunday often find any number of angry voice mails waiting for them on Monday. But those calls are the exception, not the rule. The vast majority of people in the pews are either confused about what to believe or longing to hear someone give voice to what they believe to be true. They are awash in a sea of relativism and looking for something real and solid to hold onto.

They're looking for that because none of us were made for doubt and disbelief. We were made for faith and for a real, loving, life-changing relationship with God. A desire for truth is written on our hearts. For all that the culture has infected the minds of some and for all the ways the Church has failed to form the minds of others, all our hearts possess that desire.

Similarly, as long as we're alive, we can't escape the questions God has placed in our souls to lead us to him: Who am I? Why was I created? For what purpose do I exist? What is happiness? How should I live in order to achieve happiness? What will happen to me when I die? Why do I suffer? Does anyone love me? What is the meaning of this world?

Those are the eternal questions. They are, in one form or another, asked by every human being in every country in every age. And if people are still coming to Mass on Sunday, it means the answers to those questions still matter to them. The culture hasn't convinced them that the answers they need can be found in money or things or even people.

People come to the Mass because they believe the Church has better answers than the culture does. They believe they need something, and they believe the Church is where they'll find it. They don't come looking for more of what the culture already gives them. They're looking for something different, something real, something true. They may struggle with what the Church offers. Some may not like it at first. They may fight it. But what the Church has to give is what they were made for. And when it is given as it should be—with charity, with hope, with faith—people respond far more positively than many priests' deepest fears lead them to believe they will.

And besides, the culture isn't entirely working against the Church. For as bleak as the cultural landscape may appear, there is much within the culture moving people towards God and disposing them to a life of deeper faith.

Modernism, for example, rightly sees that man has a great and unique dignity in creation. It also rightly recognizes the power man's reason has in shaping the universe. Likewise, post-modernism's critique of reason, knowledge, and progress has some merit. Reason alone is never enough. Knowledge is about more than facts. Progress is not inevitable. These are all attitudes embedded in contemporary Catholics' thinking about the world that priests can tap into and use as springboards for preaching the Gospel.

Similarly, both modernism and post-modernism encourage people to do good and improve one's community. Those are noble instincts, and when matched with a rightly ordered understanding of what "doing good" is and what "improving one's community" means, good fruit can result. The post-modern interest in "spirituality," hazy as that term may be, also has predisposed people to hearing truths not measured by the scientific method. A great many people have figured out that what they've been told will make them happy actually won't. So they're looking elsewhere. Granted, they may be looking more for something that makes them feel good than something that asks them to sacrifice, but the desire for something more is there. Priests just have to tap into that and direct it to its proper end.

The same goes for the confusion and feelings of being overwhelmed that many bring with them to Mass. It's not necessarily a bad thing for people to feel overwhelmed by the information and knowledge coming at them each day. Nor is it terrible for them to feel a bit lost in the sea of great world events or incapable of meeting all the demands on their time and energy. Each of those feelings is an opportunity for them to be awakened to the grandeur and majesty of God. It's an opportunity for them to recognize that they are not the center of the universe any more than they are capable of re-creating Eden.

There is so much pain in the world today. No priest who spends any time at all in the confessional can fail to see that. Self-doubt and self-hatred war against mistrust and unbelief. People have hurt themselves and the people they love through the terrible choices they've made. Others have been hurt by those who should have protected them—their spouses, their parents, their priests. The Church is bloody with wounds. But it's that very woundedness that brings people to their knees. It's pain that leads them to cry out to God and look for help.

The Church has wounds a plenty today, but she is also the only one capable of binding up those wounds in her members. The pain her children bear is her greatest sorrow. But it's also her greatest opportunity. Where there is woundedness, there is also need. There is a longing to be helped, healed, and redeemed. As St. Paul assures us, where sin abounds, grace abounds all the more. That tells us that we live in a time of great grace. The culture is unwittingly pulling out all the stops to bring people to the point where they are crying out for answers, where they are crying out for help. The challenge for the Church is to be there when that cry is raised.

## A HOMILETIC DIALOG

Vatican II called the Church to dialogue with the world. And a dialog is not a lecture. It involves close, attentive listening. It presupposes a deep desire to understand what the other party in the dialog is saying. It implies a relationship and a shared desire to move forward together towards truth.

The homily is, in many ways, that dialog in miniature. It is Christ speaking to his people, giving them insight into his love, his hopes, and his desires for their life. For the priest to preach *in persona Christi*, he has to look upon his congregation as Christ looks upon them—with love and understanding, fully realizing the problems and opportunities before him. He needs to see his people clearly. Knowing he needs to earn and keep earning their attention, knowing that their knowledge of Christ and his Church is rarely what it should be, knowing that their view of the world is shaped by modernity and post-modernity, and knowing that, despite all that, they still desire truth, opens up the channels of communication between priest and congregation.

Those pieces of knowledge are the stepping stones to relevance. They're points of entry for the Gospel message the priest is called to preach. Together, they create the possibility of homilies that can break through the cultural cacophony of information, that can capture and hold the congregation's attention, making it possible for them to hear the one message that truly matters. They also create the possibility of homilies that address the real crisis of catechesis and faith currently plaguing the Church, and that can re-shape Catholics' worldview according to the mind of the Church, not the culture. Finally, they create the possibility of homilies that can answer the deepest questions people bring with them to the liturgy, homilies that open people's hearts and minds to the graces of faith poured out during the Holy Sacrifice of the Mass. The bishops most recent statement *Preaching the Mystery of Faith: The Sunday Homily,* is intended for priests, deacons, and seminary formation teams and educators who prepare them to preach the Sunday homily in these times of confusion and relativism. For this reason the statement gives special attention to the biblical and theological foundations for effective liturgical preaching. It considers the proper integration of liturgy and catechesis into the Sunday homily.

What that knowledge ultimately creates is the possibility of homilies that can have real meaning for the listeners gathered—meaning now and meaning for a life yet to come.

⚬⚬⚬

I've known a lot of fathers in my lifetime. I've known fathers of big families and small families, fathers who had high paying jobs and fathers who barely managed to put food on the table, fathers who played ball with their sons and fathers who had tea parties with their daughters. Funny, serious, smart, slow, rich, poor: in the end, none of those things mattered. They didn't determine what kind of father the man was. They didn't make or break his relationship with his children. What did matter was that the father knew his children and loved his children.

The fathers who understood their offsprings' strengths and weaknesses, who knew what their children really wanted and what really made them happy, who got what made them "tick"— those were the fathers who could, in fact, father. That knowledge enabled them to give their children the help and guidance they needed. It enabled them to direct their children to the right ends by the right ways. It made it possible for them to love their children as they needed to be loved. And that made all the difference.

In the spiritual realm, fatherhood is still fatherhood. Spiritual fathers who know their spiritual children, who understand all they're struggling with and hoping for, are the kind of spiritual fathers who can lead the souls in their charge to their right end: heaven. That is where priests need to lead their congregations. That is where their homilies need to point them. That is why knowledge of the congregation gathered matters and matters eternally.

# 3

## The Liturgical Foundation:
## The Sacred Soil of Catholic Homiletics

"God: The Original Love Connection." "Rapture Threat Level: Orange."
"No Shirt, No Shoes, No Salvation." "Evil Women of History: From Jezebel
to Janet Reno."

No, none of those are real sermon titles. They're actually the sermons
announced on the billboard of the First Church of Springfield, Homer
Simpson's fictional church on *The Simpson's*. But, parodies that they are,
none of those titles would be that out of place on the billboard of the
Protestant church not too far from the seminary where I teach.

Every Sunday there's some pithy title posted on that church's marquee
advertising the pastor's upcoming sermon. And every Sunday, people
come—Bibles, notebooks, and pens in hand—to learn more about the
advertised topic. The sermon is what draws them in. It is, in fact, what the
entire worship service is built around: The Scriptures read, the songs sung,
and the extemporaneous prayers prayed are all tailored to illustrate the
issues raised in the sermon, issues chosen each week by the pastor himself.
That is exactly why the pastor (or his marketing team) invests about as
much thought and energy as the writers of *The Simpson's* do in coming up
with clever titles and taglines to post on their marquee: They have to give
people a reason to show up.

In the Catholic Church, it works just the opposite way. It is the liturgy
that shapes the homily. It is the liturgy that gives Catholic preaching its
context. It is the liturgy that gives people a reason to show up. The homily
is important, very important, but as the U.S. Bishops tell us, the homily's
"primary purpose is to be found in the fact that it is, in the words of
the Second Vatican Council, 'a part of the liturgy itself' (*Sacrosanctum*

*concilium*, 52). The very meaning and function of the homily is determined by its relation to the liturgical action of which it is a part."[1]

That's why a better Catholic homiletics is inextricably bound up with liturgical reform. If the liturgy isn't fully or rightly understood, neither can the homiletic act, whose "meaning and function" is determined by the liturgy, be fully or rightly understood. Conversely, a rightly ordered understanding of the liturgy gives rise to a rightly ordered homily, while a rightly ordered homily cultivates the soul so that it can understand and receive the graces of the Mass. The relationship is symbiotic, each aiding the other, each unleashing grace. The liturgy, however, comes first. Upon its foundation, a homily is built.

## THE SPIRIT OF THE LITURGY

In his book *The Spirit of the Liturgy*, then Cardinal Joseph Ratzinger compared the Church's liturgy to a beautiful fresco, preserved from damage, but overlaid with whitewash. According to Ratzinger, for a brief moment in the middle of the twentieth century, the Liturgical Movement and the Second Vatican Council laid the "fresco" bare, removing the whitewash and revealing its original beauty. But no sooner did people glimpse its forms and colors than did environmental hazards and restoration efforts start endangering it. The original forms were, at times, obscured. At other times, misinterpreted. The meaning, the importance of the thing, was disappearing.

Ratzinger's book outlined a strategy for arresting that process, reversing misguided restoration efforts and preserving the liturgy without whitewashing it. At its most basic, that strategy requires a clear understanding of the Mass as the fundamental prayer of the Church, where the heart of Catholic life, the Eucharist, is realized day after day. More specifically, it requires the recovery of essential beliefs about and practices within the Mass, beliefs and practices undermined or neglected in the wake of Vatican II.

That recovery has profound implications not just for the way the Mass is offered, but also for liturgical preaching. The misinterpretation and misapplication of the five pillars of Vatican II—*aggiornamento*, *ressourcement*, holiness, dialogue, and ecumenical—meant that many of the beliefs which gave preaching meaning, purpose, and context were, both in theory and practice, separated from homiletics. And, like a plant cut off from its root system, Catholic preaching suffered from that separation.

Accordingly, affecting a reform of Catholic homiletics requires reconnecting preaching to its proper liturgical roots. It requires a renewed understanding of what the Sacred Liturgy is and does. That renewed understanding begins with the liturgy's origins.

## Content and Continuity

The most fundamental teaching the Church holds about the Mass is this: The Mass is not a thing of our own making. It is God's gift to us. It is where believers gather to worship God. But, even more fundamentally, it is Christ's prayer for his Bride, his Body. Those prayers are prayed *in persona Christi* by the priest, but the words he prays are God's, given to the Church through the workings of the Holy Spirit. As such, liturgy is never ours to do with as we will. It is God's, and we have a sacred obligation to do within it only what he wills. As Pope John Paul II told the U.S. Bishops in 1998, the priest is "the servant of the liturgy, not its inventor or producer."[2]

Two thousand years ago, St. Paul illustrated that point in his letter to the Corinthians when he precisely transmitted the form of the Eucharistic liturgy, drawing from Christ's words of institution at the Last Supper.

> For I received from the Lord what I also delivered to you, that the Lord Jesus on the night when he was betrayed took bread, and when he had given thanks, he broke it, and said, "This is my body which is for you. Do this in remembrance of me." In the same way also the cup, after supper, saying, "This cup is the new covenant in my blood. Do this, as often as you drink it, in remembrance of me." (1 Cor. 11:23–26)

Note how Paul insists upon the continuity of Christ's words, his words, and the words the community is to pray: "For I received from the Lord what I also delivered to you" (1 Cor. 11:23–26).

That insistence was explained by Ratzinger in *The Spirit of the Liturgy*, when he wrote, "Man himself cannot simply 'make' worship . . . Real liturgy implies that God responds and reveals how we can worship him. In any form, liturgy includes some kind of institution. It cannot spring from imagination, our own creativity."[3]

In other words, the liturgy only has meaning—it only can be a real act of communication between man and God—because it comes from God. It is God showing us how to worship him and why to worship him so that we don't end up worshipping ourselves like the Israelites dancing around a golden calf.[4]

In tandem with a need to recognize the "givenness" of liturgy, it's also essential to recognize the continuity of the liturgy in history. The Mass we pray today, while it may differ in specific details, is, in its most basic structure, the Mass that Christians have always prayed. The Mass isn't just a liturgy for our time. It is a liturgy for all times.

Consider this passage from the letter St. Justin Martyr wrote to the Roman emperor in AD 155, describing what took place in the Christian Mass:

> The memoirs of the apostles and the writings of the prophets are read . . . When the reader has finished, he who presides over those gathered admonishes and challenges them to imitate these beautiful things . . . Then someone brings bread and a cup of water and wine mixed together to him who presides over the brethren. He takes them and offers praise and glory to the Father of the universe, through the name of the Son and the Holy Spirit and for a considerable time he gives thanks (in Greek: *eucharistian*) that we have been judged worthy of these gifts. When he who presides has given thanks and the people have responded, those whom we call deacons give to those present the "eucharisted" bread, wine and water and take them to those who are absent. (CCC 1345)

Word. Interpretation of the Word. Actualization of the Word. That is and always has been the content and structure of Catholic worship. Languages change. New missals and new translations are issued. Understanding deepens of how the precise formulations of the liturgy developed. But the heart of the liturgy never changes. It remains, like the Church herself, the same, always and everywhere, before councils and after councils. And when a priest prays the words of consecration, as much as when he preaches the homily, he prays and preaches in continuity with two thousand years of Catholic praying and preaching. He never stands alone.

## With Whom and To Whom

This brings us to the next essential point about the liturgy that must inform homiletics: It's not simply history that stands with us in the liturgy, but all the hosts of heaven as well.

In the liturgy, we look forward to eternity, to a time when we will worship God with the saints and angels, face to face. But the Mass is a participation in, as well as an anticipation of, the heavenly liturgy. When the faithful gather to worship, the veil between heaven and earth is, so to speak, drawn back. The heavens are opened, and the eternal enters into the temporal. Ratzinger writes: "The Eucharist is an entry into the liturgy of heaven; by it we become contemporaries with Jesus Christ's own act of worship, into which, through his body, he takes up worldly time and straightway leads it beyond itself, snatching it out of its own sphere and enfolding it into the Communion of eternal love."[5]

The connection between the earthly liturgy and heavenly liturgy is illustrated in the Book of Revelation, where the Apostle John is taken up into heaven and given a glimpse of the worship that takes place around the throne of God. There, he sees a group of consecrated celibate men singing a song of praise to the Lord (Rev. 14:2–4). He also sees an angel incense the altar, with the incense symbolizing the prayers of the saints (Rev. 8: 3–4). Under that altar, "are the souls of those who had been slain for the word of God and for the witness they had borne" (Rev. 6:9).

To a Catholic who attends Mass regularly, John's vision—dragons and beasts excepted—should sound familiar. That's because what John sees is what every Catholic sees at every Sunday Mass: A consecrated, celibate man—a priest—worshipping God in liturgical chant, incensing God's altar, and praying above that altar, which should contain underneath or within it the relics of a martyr or saint.

What John hears should sound equally familiar.

First, there are the antiphonal chants: "Holy, holy, holy is the Lord God almighty"; "To him who sits upon the throne and to the Lamb be blessing and honor and glory and might forever"; "Salvation belongs to our God and to the Lamb" (4:8–11; 5:9V–14; 7:10–12). There is also the *Gloria* in 15:3–4, and the Alleluia in 19:1, 3, 4, 6. There's the command to "Lift up your hearts" ("Come up hither") from Revelation 11:12, and the *Sanctus* found 4:8. Then there is the Great Amen in 19:4 and 22:21, and the celebration of the Marriage Supper of the Lamb in 19:9, the Supper announced with the words "Blessed are those who are invited to the marriage supper of the Lamb."[6]

Again and again the Book of Revelation drives home the point that the worship of the faithful on earth is intimately bound up with the worship of the faithful in heaven: The heavenly hosts offer the same worship. And they offer it to the same person: The Lamb of God.

In the heavenly vision described in Revelation, John sees the saints gathered around the Lamb. Their vision is directed towards him. Their songs of praise are about him. Their whole orientation—of body, mind, and spirit—is him, the Lamb standing as though slain.

Revelation makes clear that Christ is the object of our worship as much as he is the author of our worship. The liturgy is not about the saints. It's not about us. It's about Christ, our alpha and omega, who alone gives meaning, purpose, and beauty to human life and human community. Union with him is what we're after. That's our primary goal, not union with the community gathered. That unity matters. It's important. But it is a consequence of our union with him, a secondary effect, and if pursued apart from him, can be neither real nor lasting.[7]

## *Actualization and Re-Presentation: The "Why" of Liturgy*

To worship Christ is to worship with the people of God gathered in a particular place and time, but it is also to worship with the people of God outside of time. It's to participate now in what we are destined to participate eternally. It's to have a taste of glory even in the most ordinary of days. That taste of glory is why keeping Christ, and not man, at the center of our worship in no way demeans the human person. In fact, it is the only possible way for man to be glorified because as the eternal enters into the temporal in the Mass, the events foretold in Revelation come to pass. They are, in effect, actualized.

"Scripture is the announcement of the Word of God," Dr. Scott Hahn writes in his book *Letter and Spirit*. "Liturgy is its actualization."[8]

In the Mass, what was prophesized and foreshadowed in Scripture comes to be. The bloody sacrifices of the Old Testament are fulfilled in the bloodless sacrifice of the New. The work hinted at by the Israelites' Passover lamb is carried out by the true Paschal Sacrifice, Jesus Christ. The Bridegroom returns. The kingdom comes. God's people worship in the New Jerusalem and the New Temple. God's saving covenant is extended to all nations and renewed in the consumption of the Lamb of God. Man becomes a new creation, dead to sin, alive in Christ.

All that happens when Christ's "once for all" sacrifice is re-presented on the altar. It's remembered just as Jesus instructed: "Do this in remembrance of me" (Lk. 22:19). The Greek word used there is *anamnesis*, and it means more than just to "recall." It means to make a past event present. That's what the Eucharist does. It makes Christ's sacrifice present continually, in every age, so that the graces of his saving death can be applied to all generations. It allows every believer to stand on Calvary, at the foot of the cross, and spiritually witness the death that bought man his redemption.

Quoting *Lumen gentium* 3, the Catechism states:

> When the Church celebrates the Eucharist, she commemorates Christ's Passover, and it is made present. The sacrifice Christ offered once for all on the cross remains ever present (cf. Heb. 7:25–27). "As often as the sacrifice of

the Cross by which 'Christ our Pasch has been sacrificed' is celebrated on the altar, the work of our redemption is carried out." (1364)

"The work of our redemption is carried out." That's what ultimately happens in the Mass for the community gathered. Through the liturgy, God's saving grace is applied to all those present. The promises of salvation history are extended and fulfilled as Love offers himself in time and space to his children. The believer's task is to accept what's being offered. When we accept that, we also accept his challenge to love in return, to move away from selfishness and towards selflessness.

Through giving himself to us, God calls each of us to become self-gift, a transformed creation, capable of living in union with one another, with his world, and with him. He calls us to make an offering of ourselves, to offer our hopes, our struggles, our fears, our very lives back to him. He calls us to holiness. That's the goal of the Mass, and that's what the Mass makes possible.

## MAKING TRUTH MANIFEST

### Sacrament and Sacramentals

The inner transformation holiness demands is primarily accomplished through the Eucharist. In the Eucharist we are brought to an encounter with the true and living God. To that moment and to a full awareness of its import, the priest is called to bring his congregation.

To do that, he has the entire liturgy at his disposal. Sacred objects and sacred architecture, sacred music and sacred words, smells and bells, gesture and posture, vestments and altar cloths, all of these point the way to an encounter with the divine. So too do the set rhythms of the liturgy, words of petition and praise rooted in Scripture and Tradition that never vary. Through what Ratzinger calls liturgy's "unspontanaity," those rhythms incarnate the unchanging heart of the liturgy and the unchanging nature of that to which liturgy points.[9]

In the wake of Vatican II, many of those sacramentals and traditional liturgical expressions of faith were mistakenly jettisoned. But if the Holy Spirit used their absence from the Mass to help release Catholics from any undue attachment to them, he also, in time, used their absence to help Catholics understand just how important sacramentals actually are.

Over the past decade, especially among younger Catholics, there has been a renewed enthusiasm for everything from Latin to Gregorian chant and chapel veils. In Masses filled with the older sacramentals and liturgical practices, they've found a sense of mystery and wonder that was missing from the Masses of their childhood. They've discovered what the Catholics who populated the long centuries before Vatican II always knew: People need to see the sacred incarnated in physical realities. Creatures of the flesh that we are, we don't just want to be told about holiness. We want to see, smell, and hear it. That's what makes it real to us.

As it turns out, the "extras" and "inessentials" turned out to be not so "extra" or "inessential" after all, and no one has recognized that more than Pope John Paul II and Pope Benedict XVI. Together, they have led the movement to reintegrate traditional sacramentals and liturgical actions back into the Mass and to do so in the way intended by the Council Fathers. Benedict in particular has led by example—resuming the practice of distributing Holy Communion to the kneeling faithful, giving Gregorian chant pride of place in the Basilica of St. Peter's liturgical music repertoire, and even occasionally saying the Mass *ad orientam*—facing Christ with the people.

Explaining the reasoning behind Pope Benedict's actions, Pontifical Master of Liturgical Ceremonies, Monsignor Guido Marini, explained:

> May it not be the case that entering into God's mystery might be facilitated and, sometimes even better accompanied by that which touches principally the reasons of the heart? Is it not often the case that a disproportionate amount of space is given over to empty and trite speech, forgetting that both dialogue and silence belong in the liturgy, congregational singing and choral music, images, symbols, gestures? Do not, perhaps, also the Latin language, Gregorian chant, and

sacred polyphony belong to this manifold language which conducts us to the center of the mystery?[10]

For priests, learning to speak "this manifold language" is an essential part of the "reform of the reform." The Mass is, of course, the Mass, regardless of whether or not there's incense or bells: Jesus still shows up and grace is still given. But the more fluent priests become at the "manifold language" of which Marini speaks, the more the liturgies over which they preside incarnate the truth about what the Mass is. Likewise, the more the truth about the Mass is incarnated, the more tools people have at their disposal to help them enter into the mystery.

Homilies bear the same responsibility. Like the music sung and the prayers chanted, homilies are also called to reflect the truth about what liturgy is and help effect what liturgy aims to effect. They should lead people into the mystery, into a sacramental encounter with Christ. Their task is to articulate and help people apply the very truths contained within liturgical actions and sacramentals. That's why the "reform of the reform" isn't just about bringing back silence and incense. It's also about integrating the very things of which silence and incense speak into liturgical preaching so that preaching, in turn, can help people see beyond the silence and incense, to the realities to which they point.

## A Prayer Within A Prayer

In the context of the Mass, the homily never stands alone. It is part of the prayer that is Catholic liturgy. It is itself a prayer, which bridges the Liturgy of the Word and the Liturgy of the Eucharist, helping people make the transition from the "Table of the Word" to the "Table of Christ's Body and Blood."

Because of that, homilies are generally more about exhortation than they are about education. Education should be a part of almost every homily: In some way the priest must always seek to explain God's Word to the people. He must strive to deepen their understanding of what the Scriptures say and the One to whom they point. But that explanation is a tool that serves the ultimate end of exhortation. Moving people to put

God's Word into practice, to live it in their own lives, to love God and truth more deeply—that's what homilies are ultimately about. They're about making palpable the riches of the Father and moving the congregation to a desire for communion with God, a desire fulfilled in the Eucharist.

The U.S. bishops explain:

> Sometimes it will be appropriate to call people to repentance for the way they have helped to spread the destructive powers of sin in the world. At other times, the preacher will invite the congregation to devote themselves to some specific action as a way of sharing in the redemptive and creative word of God. However, the response that is most general and appropriate "at all times and in every place" is the response of praise and thanksgiving (Eucharist).[11]

The homily brings people to that response by helping them grasp the greatness of God's mercy and love, as well as how much hinges on their response to his call. It also accomplishes that by presenting truth—truth about God, man, grace, sin, heaven, earth. That truth paves the way for an encounter with Truth himself—a personal, incarnational, enfleshed encounter that follows immediately on the heels of the homily.

## The Liturgy-Centered Homily

The Mass, informed by a full understanding of what liturgy is—God given, linked in continuity to the past, a participation in the worship of the angels and saints, oriented to Christ and not the community, the actualization of the promises of salvation history, and the re-presentation of Christ's sacrifice on Calvary—helps people more fully and consciously encounter Christ. A homily informed by those same beliefs does the same.

For example, when a priest recognizes that the liturgy is God-given, not man made, and that he preaches *in persona Christi* just as he consecrates bread and wine *in persona Christi*, he also recognizes that he must preach with the mind of the Church, not simply with his own mind. The message he gives is Christ's message and the prayer he articulates is Christ's prayer. If a priest understands this, the homily can't be about him. It can only be about God's Word—expressed in Scripture and Tradition—and what it has to say to men and women today.

An understanding of the continuity in the liturgy likewise acts as a check on any tendency to falsely conceive of a "pre-conciliar" and "post-conciliar" Church. It grounds the priest firmly in the stream of Catholic Tradition, connecting him to the past and enabling him to draw freely from the accumulated wisdom of history, from the Fathers and scholastics to the *nouvelle* theologians of the Council years and the new apologists of today.

Similarly, knowing that the liturgy celebrated in his parish church on an ordinary Sunday is actually a participation in the heavenly liturgy, gives the priest his liturgical coordinates. It helps him grasp that when he preaches, he's not just standing in the pulpit, but in the threshold between heaven and earth. Like Hermes, the Greek deity entrusted with delivering the messages of the gods to man, the priest acts as a sort of divine messenger, passing on what he has received in prayer and study, and using humor, wit, and persuasion to open men's eyes and ears to eternal truths. The priest isn't an oracle any more than he is a minor Greek god with winged sandals, but when he speaks with the heart and mind of the Church, he delivers a message far more important and true than any message ever delivered by the mythological Hermes. He is truly the bearer of Good News.

When the priest sees the veil drawn back between the heavenly and the earthly, he also clearly sees who the proper object of worship is: Christ. With his eyes fixed on Christ, he seeks to fix the congregation's eyes there as well, pointing them away from himself and to the one he represents. Bringing people to an encounter with Christ—a personal, transforming relationship that colors everything in their lives—becomes his primary objective in the homily.

Accomplishing that objective is made all the easier by his understanding of the Mass as the realization of God's covenantal promises and the re-presentation of Christ's sacrifice. He knows what he's asking people to do: Accept the grace being offered. And he knows how he must ask them to do it: Make an offering of themselves, joining the sacrifice of their life to Christ's own sacrifice.

That, of course, requires much more of believers than just being "nice." It requires that they struggle against sin and strive for virtue. It requires that they turn to Christ and open their hearts to the graces offered in the sacraments. And it requires that they carry Christ's Good News out into the culture, that they live the mystery actualized in the Mass every minute of every day. They are to think like Christ, live like Christ, and love like Christ. When the priest knows *that* is God's desired end for every single person sitting in the pews before him, and understands that it's his responsibility to help them see that end and pursue it, he preaches not only with greater urgency, but also with greater substance. The homily becomes a true teaching moment, where Scripture, understood through the lens of Tradition and applied by the priest, becomes the guide God intended it to be.

⌇⁚⁓

A homiletics informed by the liturgy is a homiletics rooted in Scripture and Tradition. It knows it is part of a sacred prayer that has been prayed for thousands of years by untold numbers of the faithful. It also knows that in the Mass the congregation stands before the threshold of eternity. It is immersed in a great mystery that can only be grasped with the eyes of faith. It seeks to draw people to that mystery, to help them enter into it. It also seeks to help the faithful recognize what is being fulfilled in their presence, to step into the stream of salvation history and receive what has so long been promised. It aims to bring people to holiness, a holiness that is impossible without the graces given in the Eucharist.

The task of the Catholic homilist is so much more than the task of a Protestant preacher because the liturgy itself is so much more. The liturgy asks more of the congregation and gives more to the congregation. But if the nature of the Mass isn't fully understood or appreciated, if—even more problematically—it isn't faithfully offered, the homily can't help but fall short of what it should be. "Every homily, because it is an intrinsic part of the Sunday Eucharist, must therefore be about the dying and rising of Jesus Christ and his sacrificial passage through suffering to new and eternal life for us. By means of that pattern, the People of God can understand their own lives properly and be able to see their own experience in the light of the Death and Resurrection of Jesus."[12]

Likewise, if the homily falls short of being what it should, the power, beauty, and mystery of the Mass can fail to make itself manifest to the congregation. Its essential glory and grandeur is never diminished, but that glory and grandeur can elude the people sitting in the pews. Their eyes can remain shut. What is truly extraordinary appears simply ordinary, and, like the ancient Jews who paid no attention to Christ when he walked among them, the congregation gathered can miss the wonders unfolding before their eyes.

And, of course, many often do.

# Part II

Construction

# 4

## Vatican II Revisited:
## A New Design for Catholic Homiletics

Every year, one of the first things I share with my homiletics students is a short essay on preaching by the Dominican priest, Father Peter Cameron. In the essay, Father Cameron recounts a story from the beginning of Acts (3:1–26).[1]

As the story goes, a man lame from birth had his friends bring him to the temple every day. But he never went in. Rather, he lay outside the temple gates, begging for alms. One day, not long after Christ's Ascension, Peter and John saw the man as they were walking towards the temple. The man saw them too. As they approached, he cast his eyes downwards and asked for alms.

Neither Peter nor John tossed a coin in his direction. Instead, they asked him to look at them. Once Peter had his attention, the apostle said, "I have no silver and gold, but I give you what I have; in the name of Jesus Christ of Nazareth, walk." He then took the man by the hand and helped him stand. Immediately, the man's legs and ankles grew strong, so strong that he not only started walking, but leaping and praising God. Peter and John then led the man into the temple for liturgy, and every person they encountered on their way was "astounded."

Father Cameron tells that story (and I pass it on to the seminarians) because it is a near perfect illustration of how a homily works and what a homily should do.

In the person of the lame beggar, we see man, wounded by sin and looking for help. And in the persons of Peter and John, we see priests, men also wounded by sin but set apart by God and empowered to give those who come to them the help they need. As Peter did, the priest has to capture people's attention: He has to help them stop focusing on themselves and become open to receiving what God has to give. Then he has to give it. What he gives isn't his own, but rather what he has received from Christ, namely the Holy Name of Jesus. And when that gift is handed on, miracles result. There is healing, joy, and faith. And that leads to prayer and praise. It leads to the New Temple, the Eucharistic Body of Jesus Christ. Likewise, for those who witness that life-giving transformation, the response is the same: astonishment.

## The Pillars of a Renewed Homiletic

Understanding, conversion, healing, joy, faith, prayer, praise: It seems like an awful lot to accomplish in under ten minutes. And it would be if the priest was simply tasked with giving a brief speech or address. But the homily is no speech, at least no ordinary one.

In the homily, the priest "breaks open the Word." "The Word" is the Bible, a book "living and active, sharper than any two-edged sword, piercing to the division of soul and spirit, of joints and marrow, and discerning the thoughts and intentions of the heart" (Heb. 4:12). "The Word" is also a person, Jesus Christ, the only Son of God, who died for love of us. Accordingly, to break open the Word is to wield a "two-edged sword." It also is to release Christ's power, Christ's life into the congregation. And that power is limitless.

The U.S. Bishops set the bar as high for priests as Luke did in Acts when they defined liturgical preaching as: "A scriptural interpretation of human existence, which enables a community to recognize God's active presence, to respond to that presence in faith through liturgical word and gesture, and beyond the liturgical assembly, through a life lived in conformity with the gospel."[2]

That's what a homily needs to accomplish. It needs to speak to God's people in such a way as to affect all that—the recognition of God, the assent of heart and mind in faith, and the desire, knowledge, and ability to live that faith in the world. A right understanding of Vatican II, the Catholic congregation, and the Sacred Liturgy form the foundation for that kind of homily. They are, in a manner of speaking, the substructure. But what about the structure itself?

Perhaps the simplest way to answer that question is to look back at the five structural pillars of Vatican II: *aggiornamento, ressourcement,* holiness, dialogue, and ecumenical. Those concepts were intended to frame the Church's dialog with the modern world. Their misinterpretation subverted that dialog. The reform of the reform aims to replace the wrong interpretation of those principles with the right ones. And that's just as true in homiletics as it is in the rest of the Church's life.

A rightly ordered understanding of *aggiornamento, ressourcement,* holiness, dialogue, and ecumenical should frame the message of Catholic homilies. They should give it shape, substance, and purpose, directing the sacred conversation between Christ and his people to its proper end. That's what will enable priests to preach as Christ would have them preach. That's what will enable them to preach as men and women today need them to preach. That's what will enable them, like Peter and John, to lead people to understanding, conversion, healing, faith, joy, prayer, and praise.

## A HOMILETICAL *AGGIORNAMENTO*

The majority of lay Catholics give God one hour a week at best: They give him Sunday morning. A minority gives more, spending somewhere between seven and fourteen hours each week attending daily Mass, making a regular Holy Hour, praying privately, and engaging in reading and study. A tiny fraction of the Catholic laity gives even more than that. But that fraction excepted, the lives of the overwhelming majority of Catholics, regardless if they give God one hour a week or twelve, are dominated by the secular culture.

That culture shapes the news they read, the challenges they confront at the office, the topics discussed at dinner parties, and what their children learn in school. It shapes their work environment, their entertainment, and, far too often, their family life. It's their world, and they don't leave it behind when they walk through the Church's doors. Into the Church, they bring all the anxieties, challenges, and questions to which life in the world gives rise.

The homily needs to take that into account by addressing the cultural situations that create those anxieties, challenges, and questions. It needs, in the correct spirit of *aggiornamento*, to throw open the window between the Church and the culture, allowing the vast wisdom of the deposit of faith to speak to those anxieties, challenges, and questions. That's the only way priests can fulfill the homiletical task given to them in *Presbyterorum Ordinis*: "[P]riests should help men to see what is required and what is God's will in the important and unimportant events of life" (6).

*Presbyterorum Ordinis* further states that when priests do this, they need to give more than general platitudes. They need to be specific: "But priestly preaching is often very difficult in the circumstances of the modern world. In order that it might more effectively move men's minds, the word of God ought not to be explained in a general and abstract way, but rather by applying the lasting truth of the Gospel to the particular circumstances of life" (4).

That statement is a direct call for priests to engage the culture as it is— sticky, complicated, polarizing issues and all. In the homily, no important topic is off-limits. Abortion, contraception, cohabitation, divorce, marriage, pornography, finances, family, vocations, loneliness, technology, time management, the secularization of the culture, the media, death, illness, suffering, war, terrorism, injustice, corruption, disorder, immigration— you name it. If it's an issue shaping conversation and life in the culture, at some point, a priest needs to tackle it in the homily.

When he tackles it depends primarily on the lectionary. Although occasionally circumstances ask him to raise an issue not directly pertaining to the readings (e.g. in the wake of a large-scale terrorist attack or a devastating natural disaster), most of the time the readings need to be the guide for what topics he tackles and when. And despite the fact that those readings were first written thousands of years ago, there's not an issue from that laundry list above to which some Scriptural passage doesn't speak.

For example, you might not find any passages in Matthew that advise against spending too much time playing video games, but Jesus' words in Matthew 6:21, "For where your treasure is, there your heart will be," certainly apply to why investing time in people, not technology, is always more important. Likewise, none of the Gospel writers directly challenge us to reflect on how the mass media shapes the way we think. But Jesus indirectly does in Matthew 16. There, he tells his disciples to think for themselves and not just go along with public opinion. He does that by first questioning them about what others say of him and then countering that question with the all important, "But who do *you* say that I am?" (vv. 13–15).

Again, there's no dilemma, issue, or struggle in this world of ours about which Scripture doesn't have something to say. The reason for that, as *Dei Verbum* explains, is that "what was handed on by the Apostles includes everything which contributes toward the holiness of life and increase in faith of the peoples of God" (8).

The Apostles may not have foreseen *Halo* or *The New York Times*, but the Holy Spirit did, and as he is Scripture's primary author, his book is relevant to all cultures in all times, including twenty-first century America. The homilist's task is to show the congregation just how relevant the Bible actually is. It's also to bring the Church's understanding of Divine Revelation to bear on the issues of the day, explaining the "what" and the "why" of the Church's teachings on the issues at hand.

That's not always easy. Some issues have to be handled more delicately than others, with consideration for the parish's younger members. Others will make people uncomfortable, angry even. Whatever the issue, a spirit of hope and charity, not condemnation and judgment, needs to permeate the homily.

Still, however difficult or challenging some issues may be, homilists have to address them. People are thirsting for answers. They're hungering for guidance. And again, most give the Church just one hour a week to deliver those answers. If the priest doesn't find a way to do that in his homily, they'll look for the answers elsewhere. Unfortunately, when they do, the chances are that the answers they find won't be the right ones. They won't be answers that give life.

## A HOMILETICAL *RESSOURCEMENT*

Shortly after his Resurrection, two of Jesus' followers encountered him on the road to Emmaus. But they didn't recognize him for who he was. Even after he spent hours talking to them about himself, explaining how all the books of the Law and Prophets pointed to him, his followers still didn't realize that their mysterious friend was Jesus. Only after the Lord sat down with them for a meal, prayed over the bread and wine, and broke the bread, did they see him for who he was.

There is a lesson for every homilist in that story. For all Jesus' expounding on the Scriptures (and since it was God himself doing the expounding, it was probably the best theological exegesis ever), that conversation still wasn't enough to open the disciples' eyes. Talking alone couldn't make them see. Something more was necessary: the Breaking of the Bread. In their Eucharistic encounter with the Risen Lord, his followers finally got it. Then they saw. Then they understood.

So too in the Mass. The homily, for all the power that can be unleashed in the breaking open of the Word, still can't accomplish what the breaking of the Bread can. In the Eucharist, grace moves in a physical, tangible way, passing from Body to body. It, not the homily, is the "summit and source" of the faith.

The task of the homily therefore is, in large part, to prepare individuals for that encounter. Like Jesus did when he explained the Scriptures on the way to Emmaus, it should lay the groundwork for an encounter with the transcendent, the infinite. That encounter is what the *ressourcement* of the Second Vatican Council sought to renew. It wanted to strengthen people's understanding of who Christ was and what a faith rooted in him meant. It also wanted to help people put that understanding into practice, enabling them to root their faith and life ever more deeply in Christ. The goal of *ressourcement* was to send people back to the Source.

So too with the homily. A homily that incorporates the principle of *ressourcement* is a homily that helps people understand who Jesus was and draws them to an encounter with him. It prepares them to receive the Eucharist, stirring their desire for Christ, helping them see their need for Christ, helping them realize their poverty without Christ.

The U.S. Bishops explain that relationship in *Fulfilled in Your Hearing*, writing: "In the Eucharistic celebration the homily points to the presence of God in people's lives and leads a congregation into the Eucharist, providing as it were the motive for celebrating the Eucharist in this time and place."[3]

This mode of homiletics also follows the model set out for the Church by Christ on the road to Emmaus, using the Scriptures as the primary source for preaching. This doesn't mean a priest can't refer to other documents or supporting materials. Effective homilies can and do employ quotes from papal documents, the saints, great literature, and even pop culture. But the starting point and the primary guidance comes from the sacred text. Only the words of Sacred Scripture can speak absolute truth to every human need and situation. Only the words of Sacred Scripture can be called "the speech of God as it is put down in writing under the breath of the Holy Spirit" (CCC 81). The same can never be said of the words devised by the homilist, Shakespeare, or the Congregation for the Propagation of the Faith. Sacred Scripture alone has that power, a power to teach, heal, and inspire. No human words, however true and faithful, can come close to doing what God's inspired Word can do.

As St. Jerome explained more than sixteen hundred years ago: "The Lord's flesh is real food and his blood real drink; this is our true good in this present life: to nourish ourselves with his flesh and to drink his blood in not only the Eucharist but also the reading of Sacred Scripture. In fact, the Word of God, drawn from the knowledge of the Scriptures, is real food and real drink."[4]

In nourishing the faithful with the written Word, the homilist prepares them to be nourished by the sacramental Word, the Word Made Flesh. One encounter paves the way for the other.

It's that encounter, that moment where the transcendent enters into time and space under the guise of bread and wine, that enables people to move away from selfishness, self-seeking pleasure, and the misguided notions of individualism plaguing our culture. God alone makes that encounter possible. But a homily founded on the principle of *ressourcement* is one of the most effective tools he has at his disposal to accomplish that.

## A HOMILETICAL CALL TO HOLINESS

The Christian life doesn't end in the Eucharist. Holy Communion is but a taste of the eternal communion God desires with each of his children in heaven. Likewise, the goal of the homily isn't just moving people to an encounter with mystery in the Eucharist, but equipping and inspiring them to live the Eucharistic mystery in the world. The laity is called, in a sense, to be missionaries of the mystery, witnessing to Christ and God's saving grace in the midst of their daily lives. And there is one way and one way alone they can do that: by becoming holy.

Calling people to holiness is a homiletic essential. A good homily never fails, in one way or another, to issue that call. It is not, as the Catechism states, simply "an exhortation to accept this Word as what it truly is, the Word of God," but also an exhortation "to put it into practice" (1349). Likewise, as *Presbyterorum Ordinis* explains, when priests preach the Gospel, "it is to conversion and holiness that they exhort all men" (4).

The call to holiness, at its most basic, is a call to Christ. It is a call to a relationship with him, to live in love with him. And to live in love with Christ is to strive to do God's will in all things, with humility, patience, trust, and deep love. None of those things are accomplished overnight. The slow unfolding of grace in one's life is usually a painful and difficult journey. The closer we grow to Christ, the more painfully aware we become of the depths of our own sin. We are wounded to our core, and because of that we must make a constant and decided effort to continue along the path to holiness.

Accordingly, the call to holiness is also a call to ongoing conversion. The homily invites people to know and love Christ, then it gives people the guidance they need to walk the path to eternal communion with him. It encourages them to make right choices and challenges them to make difficult choices, laying out the tenets of true discipleship. In the homily, the Sacred Page becomes the launching pad for helping people understand the importance of regular prayer, pious devotions, charitable giving, frugality, forgiveness, self-denial, and ascetical practices such as fasting, chastity, and self-mortification. It also helps them understand the nature of sin, the different forms of sin, and how to tackle those sins in their daily lives.

The homily doesn't do that to inflict any sort of Catholic guilt complex on the congregation. It is always love that motivates preaching on sin and conversion. Nevertheless, no one can progress in the spiritual life without first discovering their own insufficiency and poverty. In order to grow closer to God, we all must come to learn that holiness is possible only because of his love, his grace. We have to recognize the depths of our own sin and grasp our inability to practice true discipleship apart from divine assistance. Learning that is never easy or pleasant, but there's no getting around it. Until we've mastered that lesson, there is no mastering anything else in the spiritual life. Accordingly, every homily that calls people to holiness must also call them to ongoing conversion and all that it entails.

And again, the reason for that call is love. People need to become holy. They need the Gospel. The Catholic faith isn't a random inventory of truth claims. It's not a system devised by men. The Catholic faith is a unified understanding of the human condition as revealed by God himself. His revelation is the source of every dogma, every doctrine, and the starting point of theology. And the only way for anyone to be truly happy is know that revelation, to know reality.

All of us now live in a fragmented world. Shards of disparate truth compete with shards of badly thought out philosophies. Traditions, habits, lifestyles, belief systems—all have been deconstructed by post-modernism. That fragmentation and isolation of truth is the source of much of the contemporary culture's angst. That angst, which oftentimes borders on despair, can only be overcome through a restored vision of a unified reality. That's true for the culture and that's true for every man and woman in the pew on Sunday morning. People find joy and peace when they find God, when they see the world as it is, and when they see themselves as they are. They find happiness when they realize that there is no need for despair, that there is always hope.

Hope. That is what the homiletic call to holiness offers man.

## A HOMILETICAL FRAMEWORK FOR DIALOG

In many ways, the problem afflicting most Catholics today is a problem of interpretation. Catholics are not interpreting the world correctly. They've bought into a bad hermeneutic, adopting a wrong way of making sense of life. Their hermeneutic for understanding reality is all too often, consciously or unconsciously, secularism, materialism, consumerism, or the all encompassing, post-modernism. What it's not is Catholicism. And that is the very problem Vatican II sought to avoid.

By calling for a dialog amongst Catholics, the Council Fathers hoped a common vision for making sense of the world and a common language for speaking to the world would result. They saw where the culture was heading, and knew that the language and framework of the pre-conciliar years was not adequate. It was not up to the task at hand. They were right.

Unfortunately, the initial misunderstanding surrounding their call for dialogue prevented the dialog that actually was taking place at many levels from working its way into the general understanding. And where the Church was not at work, the culture was, reshaping both clergy and laity's worldview in ways often contrary to the truth.

Accordingly, homilies today need to be a corrective to that problem. In one way or another, they need to give people the right tools for interpreting the world. They need not only to provide the faithful with the Catholic perspective on the issues of the day, but also with a framework for understanding those issues. In other words, explaining what the Church teaches—its position on abortion, pornography, or just war—is never enough. It's also necessary to give people the reasons for those teachings, the underpinnings of Catholic doctrine.

That starts with passing on a vision of a world created and governed by an all-knowing, all-loving, all-powerful God, a God who died for man and who now calls man into a personal relationship with himself. That vision also encompasses man, a creature possessing a dignity surpassing everything else in creation. But it doesn't end there. A homily that provides a framework for dialog also needs to reshape how Catholics think about the relationship between faith and reason, as well as truth and love, helping people understand that, contrary to what the world tells them, neither is mutually exclusive from the other. Faith is inherently reasonable and reason reaches its fullness only when paired with faith. Likewise, love without truth is no real love, and truth without love always rings hollow.

Homilies can also counter the culture's glorification of material happiness and self-seeking pleasure by presenting the necessity of sacrifice, the reasons for suffering, and the fruits born through self-denial. A call to reject skepticism and learn trust, to see order instead of chaos, to reject relativism and think in absolutes, to reconceive "progress" from a heavenly perspective, to recognize that God's wisdom is different from man's wisdom, to admit and accept our own limitations, and to reject earthly conceptions of happiness while embracing an eternal understanding of joy—all of that is proper to homiletics today. It's also necessary.

"Faith," *Fulfilled in Our Hearing* tells us, "can be defined as a way of seeing or interpreting the world. The way we interpret the world, in turn, determines the way we relate to it."[5]

No homily can call people to faith without also calling people to a correct way of interpreting the world. We live in philosophically dark times. People aren't bad. Most want to be good. They want to do the right thing. Especially those who've made the effort to come to Mass. But many don't know what good is. Their understanding of "the right thing" has been shaped by the culture. And they've grown complacent in that worldview.

Homilists today have to shake people out of that complacency. They need to challenge the secular worldview that impinges upon how even faithful Catholics live and think. They must push people out of their comfort zone, encouraging them to think more clearly and deeply about their lives and the world in which they live. As "debtors to the truth of the Gospel," they have to give people the framework for life and thought that the Fathers of the Second Vatican Council wanted them to have. From the pulpit they have to facilitate the dialog necessary for Catholics to stop being engaged by the world and start engaging it.[6]

## A HOMILETICAL UNDERSTANDING OF ECUMENICAL

We read in *Presbyterorum ordinis*: "Also, Christians should be taught that they live not only for themselves, but, according to the demands of the new law of charity; as every man has received grace, he must administer the same to others. In this way, all will discharge in a Christian manner their duties in the community of men" (6).

The community of men. That's who the Second Vatican Council wanted to reach. It wanted the Church's maternal care for people of every race, color, and creed known. It also wanted individual Catholics to make that care known through all their interactions, big and small, in the world. It wanted that for Catholics because in that care, in that orientation to others, the Christian life is lived.

God, John tells us, is love. He is a family, a communion of Three Persons, each perfectly giving and perfectly receiving love. That love isn't simply an emotion. It's total self-gift. And when God calls us to holiness, he calls us to become like him: to become a partaker in the Divine Nature and to become love through making a gift of ourselves.

Importantly, that gift must be given to believers and unbelievers alike. When we accept the gift of faith, we can't just pocket something for ourselves, and let those who refuse the gift go off on their merry way. Rather, we must accept the task of living for those others, of making ourselves available to serve them. To do that, we need to reject selfishness and the post-modern tendency to see the world simply from our own perspective. We must reject our egos and all their vain and proud demands so that we can understand others' needs and concerns, their questions and worldview. We must open our hearts in friendship and understanding to all those different from ourselves and through that we're able to move in love towards communion with God *and* men.

When that call to love and live for others is woven into a homily, it reflects the true ecumenical spirit of Vatican II. It calls people out of themselves and into a world that is desperate for witnesses. It reminds people that they have an obligation to their fellow man and that all their interactions, with friends and strangers alike, must be permeated with love.

Love, however, is more than saying kind words or doing corporal works of mercy. It is giving everything we have and are to our brothers and sisters. And what we have includes our faith. To have great wealth and refuse to share it with the needy is a sin against charity. To have an abundance of food and refuse to share it with the hungry is a sin against charity. And to have the most precious of treasures, the Catholic faith, and refuse to share it with the spiritually impoverished is likewise a sin against charity.

In *Evangelii Nuntiandi*, Pope Paul VI wrote that "The Church exists to evangelize." Helping Catholics see that and know that those words are meant for them as much as for their priests and bishops, as well helping them understand the difference between evangelization and proselytization, are both tasks proper to the homily. Remember, *Fulfilled in Our Hearing* stresses that the goals of liturgical preaching reach "beyond the liturgical assembly" to "a life lived in conformity with the gospel." The ultimate goal of Catholic preaching is a love-transformed mankind and a love-transformed world. And only when Catholics fully and freely share their faith, through word and deed, can that goal be accomplished.[7]

## UNLEASHING GRACE

If homilists want their preaching to accomplish what Peter and John accomplished so long ago in Jerusalem, if they want their preaching to unleash the powers and graces of Christ, the Word of God, into their congregations, their homilies must be built upon the pillars of *aggiornamento*, *ressourcement*, holiness, dialogue, and an ecumenical spirit of charity.

The homiletical message must engage the issues that affect people the most, no matter how challenging addressing those issues might be. The message must also point souls to Christ, both in Word and Sacrament, making real the mystery of both and increasing desire for an encounter with Christ in the Eucharist. It must call people to holiness, to a life-changing, life-giving relationship with Christ. It must impart a Catholic worldview to the congregation, helping them see the world and their place in it with

Catholic eyes. And lastly, it must move them to love, a love understood not as the world understands it, but as God lives it.

When homilies do that, they can't help but be homilies that evangelize . . . which they're supposed to be: "Its character should be that of a proclamation of God's wonderful works in the history of salvation, the mystery of Christ, ever made present and active within us, especially in the celebration of the liturgy" (*Sacrosanctum concilium*, 35).

Likewise, when homilies do that, they can't help but be homilies that catechize . . . which, again, they're supposed to be: "By means of the homily the mysteries of the faith and the guiding principles of the Christian life are expounded from the sacred text, during the course of the liturgical year" (*Sacrosanctum concilium*, 52).

Above all, when homilies' messages are structured around those five pillars, they can't help but be homilies which inspire people to know, love, and live their faith . . . which, of course, is what they're supposed to be: "Ministers of the divine word . . . [should] provide the nourishment of the Scriptures for the people of God, to enlighten their minds, strengthen their wills, and set men's hearts on fire with the love of God" (*Dei Verbum*, 23).

Not every homily will give equal time and weight to all five pillars. Nor will they always evangelize, catechize, and inspire directly. Different occasions and different passages from Scripture will lend themselves differently to different tasks. But to a certain degree, *aggiornamento*, *ressourcement*, the call to holiness, dialogue, and an ecumenical perspective, should be present in every homily, as should the goals of evangelization, catechesis, and inspiration. That is what is needed in the Church today. And that is how Pope Benedict XVI, John Paul II, the U.S. Bishops, and the Fathers of Vatican II have long been asking priests to preach.

⌇

Again and again Pope Benedict XVI has said that if the art of living remains unknown, nothing else is possible.[8] The only way man can truly come to know the art of living is through an encounter with Christ. The Mass is the place where that encounter, on earth, happens in the fullest and most meaningful way possible. And the homily is where that encounter should be explained and facilitated. It should be, in effect, where the art of living is taught. It should be where the most fundamental questions of human existence are answered. It should be and can be the place where the light of truth is shone brightly and powerfully on the muddy, murky mess of modern life.

# 5

## The Builders of a New Homiletics:
## Priests, Prophets, and Fathers

Father Augustine (Gus) Donovan, T.O.R., was a lot like E.F. Hutton. When he talked, people listened.

Standing barely 5'4" Father Gus was a round little Irishman who bore more than a passing resemblance to a leprechaun. He had the personality of a leprechaun too, causing impish but harmless mischief wherever he went. If you got too close, you risked getting snapped with his Franciscan cord or pelted with a snowball. It was also, at least according to Father Gus, always his birthday. "Aren't you going to wish me a happy birthday?" or "Today's my birthday and nobody remembered," were stock phrases for the priest, and when they were used on unsuspecting souls, the result was usually the delivery of birthday cakes to the friary where he lived.

Attending Father Gus' dogma classes was like being on a retreat. Every class was a spiritual experience. Inside class or outside of class, Father Gus' sense of humor was lively, his wit quick, his wisdom penetrating, and his faith great enough to move mountains. Nobody who met him forgot him. Nor did they forget the homilies he preached. They were direct and to the point but embedded in tenderness. If there was anything Father Gus never skimped on, it was truth. He preached fatherly on the topics other priests shied away from—meaninglessness, affluenza, man's inhumanity, egocentrism, existential guilt, self-hatred, addictions—and he did it without flinching.

Father Gus' droll sense of humor could occasionally work its ways into a homily. If he saw seminarians or other young people not paying attention or growing fidgety, he would solemnly proclaim but with tongue in cheek, "If you look at your watch, may you fail your next exam." But on the whole, there was very little joking from Father Gus in the pulpit. He was never trying to put on a show nor was he appealing to mere human respect. He understood the sacredness of the task he undertook every time he stepped into the pulpit, and his preaching reflected that.

If he wanted to, Father Gus could preach for an hour without losing his listeners' attention. But he didn't. Instead, he kept his homilies short, never speaking longer than was necessary to get his point across. One weekday, he walked into the pulpit, glared at the congregation, and simply said, "As this Gospel proclaims negative humor is from the pit of hell. Leave it there." Then, he turned right back around and sat down. To this day, no one who heard that homily has forgotten one word of it. Nor have they been able to engage in any negative humor—mean-spirited teasing, making fun of someone, etc.—without Father Gus' interpretation of that passage of Scripture coming back to challenge them.

The same can be said for any number of other transgressions. Every time Father Gus preached, he preached as an invitation for conversion. People walked away with a deepened understanding of themselves, sin, Christ, grace, virtue and the Christian life. His homilies were convicting. They were evangelical, catechetical, inspirational—everything a homily is supposed to be. And they were that way not just because of the words he preached, but because of the Christ he encountered in the Scriptures and the life he lived. People listened and were pastorally converted because of the homilist he was.

## The Importance of Character

What was true for Father Gus is equally true for all called to preach the Word of God: The content of a man's character has a profound effect on how the content of his homily is received. Who a priest is matters. It makes him a more effective preacher. It molds the way he prepares to preach. It molds the words he preaches. And it molds the way people listen to what he preaches.

The historical, cultural, and liturgical context of the homily form the foundation for a renewed homiletics. A correct understanding of *aggiornamento, ressourcement,* holiness, dialogue, and ecumenical—

integrated and applied—shapes its structure, message, and content. But a strong foundation and smart design are never enough. Something more is required. The building plans have to be executed. The materials have to be put together.

And that's where the character of the priest comes into play. In today's world, words alone are never enough. Few people automatically trust their priest anymore. More often than not, they're skeptical of those who claim spiritual authority, and they're on the lookout for any traces of empty religiosity. Their hypocrisy antenna is finely tuned. Accordingly, perhaps more than ever before, it is of the utmost importance that preachers of the Word not only preach *about* God, but also preach *with* God. That's what Father Gus did, and that's why precious few souls escaped one of his homilies without being touched by the words he proclaimed.

Now, unlike Father Gus, most priests I know can't get away with lying with abandon about our birthdays. We're not all leprechauns nor should we be. God calls men of all stripes to receive Holy Orders, and what works for some will most definitely not work for others. Regardless, there are certain essential characteristics or habits that all priests, regardless of personality, must strive to develop if they want to preach effectively. There are, in fact, at least nine, starting with an understanding of vocation.

## A MAN SET APART

Priests are not like other men. Of course they have many of the same needs, desires, hopes, and fears. They have interests and habits very much like their non-priestly brothers. But they still are not like other men. And that is because of the mark God places on their souls when they receive the Sacrament of Holy Orders.

That mark confers upon them the ability to minister the sacraments. It also confers upon them a special responsibility to preach God's Word.

Priests "have the primary duty of proclaiming the Gospel of God to all," says *Presbyterorum Ordinis* (4). Likewise, adds the Catechism, "They [priests] are consecrated in order to preach the Gospel" (1564).

By proclaiming the Word of God, both documents mean much more than delivering the Sunday homily. But both also place special emphasis on liturgical preaching.

Quoting *Sacrosanctum concilium*, the U.S. bishops explain, "A key moment in the proclamation of the Gospel is preaching, preaching which is characterized by the 'proclamation of God's wonderful works in the history of salvation, that is the mystery of Christ, which is made ever present and active within us, especially in the celebration of the liturgy.'"[1]

A priest must never forget how sacred of a responsibility preaching is. When a man answers the call to the priesthood, he accepts that responsibility. And to neglect that responsibility—either by failing to prepare adequately to preach, by shying away from difficult subjects, or by failing to proclaim the fullness of truth in the homily—is to neglect his vocation.

Likewise, a priest must never reduce preaching to a mere job or function. Preaching isn't just something he does. It's an integral part of who he is. Accordingly, to live his priestly identity, to be faithful to the call to proclaim the Gospel, he must guard the distinctiveness of that identity.

On the one hand, that means that the priest must live, at least in some ways, as a man set apart, striving to think and act with the mind of God. That requires renouncing certain pleasures and desires. It requires giving up things both big and small. It requires that he understand the culture, but never let himself be controlled by it. The passions of the world must never consume the priest or color his thinking. He needs to see the world for what it is so that he can name the sins afflicting it and name the grace that it needs at that moment. And if he's not living as a man set apart, it will be the world, not the Catholic faith, that eventually becomes the primary force shaping both his priesthood and his preaching.

Guarding the distinctiveness of the priestly call also requires cherishing and respecting the difference between the priesthood and the lay vocation. While the laity is also called to preach the Gospel, the call is different in kind from that of the priest. The call to proclaim God's Word is at the heart of a priest's identity. Millstones are his fate if he leads people astray, whether through his own preaching or through surrendering his sacred responsibilities. As such, he has the greater obligation and the greater burden. He can't leave the heavy lifting on evangelization, catechesis, and spiritual formation to his lay staff. He can't take the easy way out, preaching pleasant and palatable messages on Sunday, while relegating the difficult teaching on difficult subjects to DREs and Adult Faith Formation Directors.

The priest can't, of course, accomplish everything in his liturgical preaching. ten minutes is hardly enough time, for example, for a through catechesis on the dignity of the human person or the sacredness of the marital act. Follow-up outside the Mass, through Bible studies, lectures, movies, and programs, is always necessary. But if the priest never preaches an idea or a doctrine during the Mass, that undermines that doctrine when it's taught outside the Mass. He has an authority and a special grace for proclaiming truth that no DRE has. Both his parishioners and his staff need him to use that authority and grace. He neglects those things to their peril and his own.

## HUMILITY

A homilist must preach with a distinct understanding of his sacred call. But he must also be careful not to confuse the dignity of that call with any merits of his own. He must be humble and preach humbly, never seeking to draw the congregation's focus to himself, but rather to point them towards Another.

A humble preacher wants the listeners to face God, not himself. He recognizes that he is not the center of the homiletical act any more than he is the center of the liturgical act. That role belongs to God and God alone. As such, he never preaches on merely his own opinions or thoughts. He preaches the wisdom of the Church. He also approaches his preparation for the homily with a desire to seek out that upon which God wants him to preach.

He does that by entering into a dialogue with God before he preaches, leaving himself open for direction from the Holy Spirit. He also does that by engaging in an ongoing dialogue with his listeners, seeking to understand where they are so that he can best meet their needs, both perceived and unperceived, through his preaching. This humility in no way limits the preacher. As Francis Fernandez wrote, "Humility doesn't clip the wings of our desires, but rather helps us understand the need to have recourse to God to make them come true."[2]

Through humility, the priest discovers he can't obtain anything truly precious merely by his own seeking. He must wait for the gifts of understanding and wisdom. He must wait for insights into the Gospel and the human heart. Humility also teaches the priest that he can't produce the effects of grace in his congregation. He can preach faithfully and true, doing his best to pass onto them what he's received from God, but then he must wait for the Spirit to act. He is merely the mediator. God is the actor.

Ultimately, humility helps a priest remember that, like his congregation, he too is a receiver. He has been given wisdom, power, and grace that are entirely and utterly unmerited. Nothing is his own. Everything is God's. All honor belongs to God. All praise belongs to God. The priest preaches out of his own poverty. But because of that what he gives his listeners comes from God's riches, and it is of far finer stuff than if it were merely his own.

## OBEDIENCE

Humility is also what makes obedience possible.

Although he was himself God, Christ humbled himself in his death. He was obedient to the will of the Father, praying "Not my will, but yours, be done" (Lk. 22:42). That obedience brought healing and redemption, reversing the curses rendered in the wake of Adam's disobedience. It also set the model for all those called to preach and teach *in persona Christi*. They too must submit their will to the Divine Will.

As *Presbyterorum Ordinis* states: "By this humility and by willing responsible obedience, priests conform themselves to Christ. They make their own the sentiments of Jesus Christ who "emptied himself, taking on the form of a servant," becoming obedient even to death (Phil. 2:7–9)" (15).

That obedience is made concrete in ecclesial obedience. Priests and deacons give the gift of obedience to their bishops. Bishops give the gift of obedience to the Pope. All give their obedience to God and truth.

Speaking of priests, *Presbyterorum* says:

> Priests, never losing sight of the fullness of the priesthood
> which the bishops enjoy, must respect in them the authority
> of Christ, the Supreme Shepherd. They must therefore stand
> by their bishops in sincere charity and obedience. This
> priestly obedience, imbued with a spirit of cooperation is
> based on the very sharing in the episcopal ministry which is
> conferred on priests both through the Sacrament of Orders
> and the canonical mission. (7)

Of course, the priest is bound to be obedient to something other than his
bishop. He is also bound to be obedient to the truth: "They are defenders of
the common good, with which they are charged in the name of the bishop.
At the same time, they are strenuous assertors of the truth, lest the faithful
be carried about by every wind of doctrine" (*Presbyterorum ordinis*, 9).

That obedience to his bishop and the truth gives a priest freedom—
freedom from arbitrariness, freedom from false teaching, and freedom
from confusing his will with God's will. It also gives his preaching
authority. When he preaches, he preaches with the weight of centuries and
saints behind him. He is not a "lone voice crying out in the wilderness," but
the ageless voice of Christ speaking through his Church.

When a priest speaks out against his bishop in a homily or when he
explicitly violates the liturgical norms of his diocese, he breaks that bond.
When a priest preaches that which is not the faith of the Church or what
actually contradicts it, he breaks that bond as well. He diminishes himself
and the words he preaches.

As long as bishops continue to be human men, priests will have just
complaints against them. And as long as human minds are tasked with
wrestling with divine truths, there will be questions of discipline or
doctrine that priests don't understand with great ease. Some that they
might even struggle with mightily. But the homily is never the place to
express those complaints or doubts. The homily is never the preacher's
personal forum. The more he sees it as such, the less effective he will be,
and the more eternal damage, to himself and others, he will do.

## PASSION FOR THE WORD

In one of her books about poetry, the poet Mary Oliver tells the novice poet that if they wouldn't die if they couldn't write poetry, they should shut the book and go no further. The only people who can become poets, she believed, were those who would die if they couldn't become one.

To a certain extent, the same can and should be said of priests. To preach God's Word well, there has to be an unquenchable passion for that Word. There must be a desire to proclaim it that trumps all other desires. The prophet Jeremiah witnesses to that.

In the twentieth chapter of the book that bears his name, Jeremiah despairs of making any difference. He wants to give up and leave the wayward sons of Judah to their well-deserved fate. But no sooner does he retreat and shut the door on God's people, than does he feel the fire to preach well up inside him again. It's a passion that he can't contain. And so he goes back out to preach once more.

That story tells us two things. First, it tells us that the passion to preach isn't of a preacher's own making. Jeremiah couldn't conjure up that passion. In fact he rebelled against it. But God poured it into his heart when it was needed most. God gave Jeremiah the fire he needed to accomplish his will. Second, that story tells us that when that passion comes, we mustn't run away from it. We mustn't fear it, and we mustn't fight it.

Time and time again I've seen my seminarians experience the first flickers of this passion, and it almost always takes them by surprise. They don't know what it is, and they don't know where it came from. Their first instinct is to run from it. They can if they want. Some priests certainly have. But it really is nothing to be afraid of. Great zeal for God's Word, an overwhelming desire to speak truth, is part and parcel of the prophetic mission in which all priests partake.

When that zeal takes hold of a priest's heart, the thing to do is embrace it, not run from it. Give in to it, seeing in it God's will to have that truth proclaimed. The more priests come to recognize that passion for what it is, the more effectively they can use it to make their homilies powerful. And while they can't produce the feeling on their own, they can nurture it. They can devote time and energy to studying God's Word, meditating on it and praying over it. They can and should memorize it, making it part of the fabric of their inner life. And they should encourage the study of it among those they minister to. The more a priest feeds the love of God's Word in others, the more it grows in his own heart, and the more clearly it comes across when he proclaims it to the people of God.

## PASSION FOR PRAYER

Karl Rahner once said that unless priests of our day become mystics, the Church will collapse in on itself.[3] He may have been overstating the case somewhat—there is, after all, that "gates of hell shall not prevail" promise—but there was still truth in his words. The Church needs her preachers to be men of prayer, deep and abiding prayer. Apparitions and stigmata aren't required, but a devotion to spending time with God, listening to God, and expressing our innermost hearts to God is.

No marriage where the husband and wife lived in silence could ever survive. Communication sustains marriage. It strengthens the marital bond and increases the couple's love for one another. So too with the relationship between the preacher and Christ. Without ongoing, loving, open communication—which is the essence of prayer—the love of the preacher for the One he serves breaks down. It grows cold and loses it early fervor.

That's even more true in today's culture. The support for those in Holy Orders is weak and rare. The temptations strong and many. The Internet and cable offer endless worldly distractions. The demands of running a parish or an institutional chapel grow greater by the day, while fewer and fewer priests have someone to share their burden with. They live alone in the rectory, and they minister alone in the Church. Unless they turn to Christ again and again in prayer, unless they foster a prayer life that is, in a sense, mystical, they place themselves in grave spiritual danger.

Likewise, if the love between the priest and the Lord grows cold, so does their preaching. The fire of love is gone. The passion to proclaim his name dies out. When love for the Lord is absent from the heart of the preacher, it can't be enkindled in the hearts of those to whom he preaches.

And if they can't see the fruits of prayer in the one who stands in the pulpit and preaches, how many will know anything of the fruits that prayer can bear in their own lives? How many will pursue a serious prayer life on their own initiative? How many will listen and put into practice what their priest advises? Some will. But many won't.

People need to see prayer modeled for them. They need to see their priest stopping by the sanctuary for visits. They need to see him in the adoration chapel. They need to see him praying the Rosary, the Chaplet, and the Stations. They need to know that their spiritual father takes his obligation to pray the Liturgy of the Hours seriously. When they see and know all that, they know they're listening to a man who believes what he says. They know they're listening to a true witness. And that, above all, is what they want their priests to be.

## REVERENCE FOR THE LITURGY

The most important prayer a priest can pray, of course, is the Holy Sacrifice of the Mass. And the way he prays it is bound up with his effectiveness as a preacher. Both the liturgy and the homily teach Catholics about their faith. Both also inspire them to live and learn their faith. But where the homily more explicitly teaches, the liturgy more explicitly inspires.

Through smells and sights and sounds, it conveys to the congregation a sense of the sacred. It draws them into a mystery that the homily, in one way or another, explicates. The more attuned a priest is to that, the more readily the congregation can become attuned to that. His reverence in the Mass confirms their own feelings of awe and wonder. It validates those right instincts. If a priest treats the Mass as something to be manipulated at will, if he appears bored and disconnected, or if he acts as if he is the center of the action, as if the Mass were all about him, that attitude is passed on to the congregation. They become not only less willing, but less able to sense the sacredness of the act in which they're participating. They, in fact, become less willing or interested in participating at all.

They also listen less to what he says in the homily. If the Mass isn't treated as a sacred prayer, why would the congregation think of the homily as a continuation of that prayer? Moreover, if the priest hasn't modeled for them a spirit of adoration throughout the liturgy, why would they allow him to lead them to a spirit of adoration?

People need to see the priest adoring Christ from the moment the entrance processional begins to the last second of the recessional. Whether he's genuflecting before the tabernacle or distributing the Sacred Host, the priest must carry out his every action with understanding and reverence. He must never forget what a great privilege has been entrusted to him. He must understand and give thanks for what God allows him to do. When he does that, the Mass does manifest itself as a prayer to the congregation. It does inspire. And it does open up the people to learning not simply through signs and symbols, but through words and the Word.

## PATIENCE

There are few small boys who haven't rolled their eyes at their mother when she solemnly intoned, "Patience is a virtue." But Mom was right. Patience is a virtue, a virtue as necessary for preaching a good homily as for getting along with your siblings.

First, patience helps the homilist prepare to preach. It helps him step back from all the competing demands on his time and rightly prioritize them. It also helps him recognize that what might seem urgent is not always importnt. Patience helps the priest find the time he needs to prepare his homily, and it reminds him that preaching effectively requires time and work, as do nearly all things that matter.

In the midst of that preparation, patience helps the priest listen to God. It teaches him that inspiration can't be summoned on demand. It too takes time. Quiet prayer and study can help, but the most important thing a preacher can do iwait and listen for God to speak. Similarly, patience enables the preacher to carefully think through his homily. It helps him try out different ways of communicating the same idea as he searches for the most fruitful and effective means of framing the homily's message.

When the preacher goes to deliver that homily, patience shapes the attitude underlying his preaching. Yves Congar once said, "Impatient men with too little awareness of Tradition, putting their pet notion before all else, are liable to turn any reform into a sectarian movement."[4] Those are words every preacher needs to take to heart. There is only so much one man can accomplish in any one homily, and pushing any agenda with too much force will often end up backfiring on him. Wars of ideas are not won overnight, and no matter how well crafted and well delivered a homily may be, there will still be some neither touched nor swayed by it. The problems afflicting individual Catholics and the Church as a whole did not originate overnight, nor will they be resolved overnight. Recognizing that prevents the priest from becoming frustrated when his words seemingly aren't heard, and keeps both bitterness and anxiety from creeping into the tone of a homily.

Finally, patience reminds the preacher that God may be using his words in ways he cannot see, that their meaning might be unfolding gradually and quietly in the corner of some listener's mind, waiting for the *kairos* moment, for God's time, to come into full flower. Ultimately, that frees the preacher to love, not to judge the souls before him, and to try unceasingly to reach them, certain that when the time is right, God will act. In other words, patience nourishes hope.

## MAKING THE GIFT OF SELF

Man's redemption was not won by words. It did not hinge upon some great rhetorical art. It was accomplished through Christ's suffering and death. It was the result of sacrifice, and the sacrifice was the self-gift of the God-Man. In the liturgy, that self-gift is perpetuated for all time. Christ gives himself daily to his people. He nourishes them with his own body. That gift says far more to the faithful about who Christ is than anything a priest can ever say. Similarly, the way a preacher lives his own life communicates far more about his faith than any homily he delivers ever can. It can add power to his words or it can make them ring hollow. That's true in many ways, but above all it's true in the realm of self-gift.

No preacher today can convince others to give up their lives for the sake of the kingdom of God unless he has first given up his own. In his sacrifice of time, comfort, and attention he communicates to people not only the fact of his self-gift, but also what it means to become self-gift. That communication happens in two primary ways.

First, it happens through his presence. The preacher needs to be present to the faith community he serves. As much as possible, he needs to be at faith formation activities, social events, and the missionary activities of the parish. Even when his presence is not required, it's helpful for him, at the very least, to make an appearance. He needs to show his support, his interest, and his enthusiasm for all the good work his staff and congregation are undertaking. He also needs to be present at the times when people need him the most: when death, illness, or tragedy strike, when marriages fall apart or teenagers rebel, and especially when sins need to be confessed. His presence in hospitals and homes, the confessional and the rectory is a living witness to God's presence, to God's readiness to listen and care for his children whenever and wherever they need him.

But it's not just presence that signifies self-gift. It's also the ability to listen. Those who met John Paul II and Blessed Teresa of Calcutta invariably said the same thing about their meeting: When the pope or the sister spoke to them, they felt as if they were the only person in the world. Those two holy people focused all their attention on the one to whom they spoke. For as long as the conversation lasted, whether it was five seconds or five hours, they were totally and completely absorbed in the other. Each relegated their own concerns to some distant corner of their mind. In those moments, John Paul and Blessed Teresa died to themselves and gave everything they had to another.

That same kind of listening is required of those who preach. They must cultivate the ability to dismiss finance council meetings and human resource woes from their minds when someone else requires their attention. They must die to themselves to be fully present to the other. That presence shapes the words a priest speaks, as well as how those words are perceived. The better a listener a preacher is, the more fully he understands those to whom he preaches. And the more he understands them, the more he can speak in a way they will understand. Only if he can truly listen, can a priest speak words that people will hear.

Both kinds of presence, physical and emotional, are far from easy. And they can be carried out with a good spirit only through constant practice. Part of that practice involves personal asceticism. Mortification of the flesh and spirit are never optional—not for any priest and not for any Christian. But the demands placed upon the priest and the obligations he shoulders require more from him.

*Presbyterorum Ordinis* states:

> In like fashion, priests consecrated by the anointing of the Holy Spirit and sent by Christ must mortify the works of the flesh in themselves and give themselves entirely to the service of men. It is in this way that they can go forward in that holiness with which Christ endows them to perfect man ... As leaders of the community they cultivate an asceticism becoming to a shepherd of souls, renouncing their personal convenience, seeking not what is useful to themselves but to many, for their salvation, always making further progress to do their pastoral work better and, where needful, prepared to enter into new pastoral ways under the direction of the Spirit of Love, which breathes where it will. (12–13)

It's between each preacher and his spiritual director to develop a plan of personal asceticism. Habits that work for one priest will do nothing for another. Certain practices that would challenge some, could threaten the health or efficacy of others. But the need for concrete and practical acts of corporal and spiritual mortification remains. When it comes to asceticism, the question for a priest is never "if." It's "how."

## KINDNESS

Not long ago, I addressed one of Pittsburgh's newest classes of deacons shortly before their ordination. I wanted my words to encourage them, but there was also a plain truth that needed speaking.

"When the stole is given to you and lowered down upon you," I told them, "it will be a source of great joy. But it also is accompanied by a great responsibility. When you become a preacher of God's Word, you must realize and understand that you are either bringing people closer to Christ or sending them farther away. You are giving them joy or providing them with a reason for sorrow. You are bringing them into the light or sending them into the darkness."

I went on to explain to them that those words apply even when they aren't wearing the stole. Because they have been ordained, everything they do, every choice they make, every word they speak, in and out of the pulpit, carries added weight. They are ambassadors of Christ in the world, and fair or not, many in the world will judge Christ by them. They also will weigh the words spoken in the pulpit against the life lived outside the pulpit. That's even more true for priests, who are always supposed to be living and acting *in persona Christi*. And it is why of all the human virtues a priest needs to cultivate, kindness may be the most important.

"In building up of the Church, priests must treat all with exceptional kindness in imitation of the Lord," the Fathers of Vatican II wrote in *Presbyterorum Ordinis*, 6.

Several paragraphs earlier they said:

> To achieve this aim, certain virtues, which in human affairs are deservedly esteemed, contribute a great deal: such as goodness of heart, sincerity, strength and constancy of mind, zealous pursuit of justice, affability, and others. The Apostle Paul commends them saying: "Whatever things are true, whatever honorable, whatever just, whatever holy, whatever loving, whatever of good repute, if there be any virtue, if anything is worthy of praise, think upon these things" (Phil. 4:8). (3)

That doesn't mean that priests should hesitate to preach or say the truth. The Council Fathers clarified their admonition to kindness by adding, "They should act toward men, not as seeking to please them, but in accord with the demands of Christian doctrine and life. They should teach them and admonish them as beloved sons" (6).

Proclaiming hard truths is unavoidable. But a desire to wound only as much as is necessary for healing must permeate all correction. Kindness must be the cornerstone. And when it is, people will listen.

∾∶∾

A priest must understand and live his vocation as a man set apart to preach. He must cultivate a spirit of humility, a self-understanding defined by a recognition that he is a servant, unworthy of the call and graces he has received. He must submit himself to his bishop and the demands of truth. He must welcome a passion for proclaiming God's Word and cultivate a passion for encountering God in prayer. He must strive for the virtue of patience. And he must live the Gospel he preaches by making a gift of himself and treating all he encounters with fatherly kindness.

When a priest cultivates those habits of virtue, he more fully and faithfully preaches the Gospel every minute of every day. He also more fully and faithfully preaches the Gospel during the Sacred Liturgy. His words, his attitude, his manner of address are all colored by those habits. And so is people's desire to hear him speak. The more trust they have in the preacher on a human level, the more willingly they'll listen to him on a spiritual level. His life will speak to them as well as his words, and in both, they'll come to see more clearly the Author of Life himself. That's the difference a master builder makes.

# 6

## Tools of the Trade:
## The Nuts and Bolts of Catholic Homiletics

Several years ago, when I served as a pastor of a large parish in Pittsburgh, I invited my friend and mentor Bishop John McDowell to speak to a group of lay volunteers about Scripture. About 150 turned out that day, so we held the lecture in the church.

Bishop McDowell started his talk with a story about his mother and how the two of them used to sit on their porch swing and read the Bible together when he was a little boy. As he told the story he moved almost imperceptibly from left to right, the movement of the swing echoing in both the rhythm of his voice and the rhythm of his body.

At the time, I was standing at the very back of the church, watching both him and the volunteers. I couldn't see their faces. But I didn't have to. I knew they were paying attention. And the reason I knew that was because as the bishop moved from left to right, so did his listeners. Back and forth, back and forth, just like the bishop himself. They were engrossed in what he was saying, forgetting themselves in the story he told. It was quite a sight.

That talk of Bishop McDowell's wasn't a homily, but it was very much like the homilies I saw him preach before and after that day. He was a master of the art of preaching, and those privileged to hear him rewarded that mastery by giving him their undivided attention. They listened, and they learned.

What made Bishop McDowell such a great homilist? What made people sit up and take notice when he began preaching? A lot of it has to do with what we've talked about thus far. The bishop had a profound understanding of what homilies are supposed to be and do. He also had a profound understanding of the people to whom he preached, not to mention a tremendous love for the Mass. Bishop McDowell was a "post-Vatican II" priest in the best sense. Not only was he committed to all the Council Fathers had set out to do in the Church, but he knew how to integrate the Council's goals and objectives into every aspect of his priestly ministry, from the way he taught and prayed to the way he offered the Mass and preached his homilies. He "got it," and that showed.

Nevertheless, I've known other priests who "got it" as well, but who couldn't touch Bishop McDowell when it came to effective preaching. In theory, they should have been more than his match. But in practice . . . not so much.

The reason for that is that homilies aren't preached in theory. They're preached in practice, and there, head knowledge only gets you so far. To preach a truly effective homily, a priest has to not just know what to say but also how to say it. He has to know how to develop a homily with a clear, concise, relevant message, and he has to know how to deliver that message in an engaging and accessible way. Execution matters, which is why Bishop McDowell was a master of the art of preaching: He was a master of execution.

Few preachers are born with that kind of mastery. It takes time, and it takes work. But it can be learned. And when it is learned, it becomes the thread that holds every other piece of the homiletic reform together. It connects them, binds them, and turns the whole into something remarkable.

So where does finding that thread begin?

With preparation.

## PREPARING A HOMILY

### Setting the Stage

To say that priests are busy men is rather like saying the pope is Catholic. It's something of an understatement. Between dealing with budgets, committees, staff, volunteers, students, parents, parishioners, local officials, and community members, a priest's days are full from before sun-up to well after sundown. Accordingly, in the midst of overseeing rummage sales, Confirmation retreats, and disputes about heating bills, it's never surprising when homily preparation gets pushed to the back burner. There is always something more urgent, more immediate demanding their attention. But, other than their own personal prayer life, there is nothing more important.

Whether it's a homily for a daily Mass or Sunday Mass, preparation is the foundation for effectiveness. It's key. Crucial. Quite literally a matter of life or death—spiritual life or death that is. Preachers owe it to God, they owe it to the people, and they owe it to themselves to deliver the best possible homily they can give, and that simply can't be done without adequate time, study, reflection, and practice. If a priest is not prepared to deliver a homily, it is almost better that he does not preach. More good is likely to come of a moment of silence than ten minutes of unfocused, unclear preaching. In fact, I tell my seminarians that if someone asks them at the very last minute to preach—say if the designated homilist doesn't make it to Mass—they should simply say, No.

No matter how busy they are, priests must carefully guard their homily preparation time. Other responsibilities need to be scheduled around homily prep, not vice versa. Just as their time for adoration, the Liturgy of the Hours, and other personal devotions are set in stone, so too should be their time for working on their homilies. The time needed for such work will vary depending on whether the homily is for daily Mass or Sunday Mass, but the time needs to be set aside and protected regardless.

In a similar manner, each priest needs to make it a priority to find a place suitable for the work of homily preparation. For some, the best place is their office. For others, it's a quiet corner of the rectory. Fulton Sheen used to write his homilies in front of the Blessed Sacrament. I've known other priests who take to the outdoors for at least some of the work. Wherever it is, it needs to be a place free from noise and distractions, a place where one can work and pray without constant interruption.

Today, places like that have become hard to find. Email and cell phones follow us wherever we go, keeping us connected, but also repeatedly pulling our attention away from where it needs to be. If a priest can find a time of day—perhaps early morning or late evening—where no sane person would be in a position to interrupt him, that's good. If he can shut down the email and shut off the cell phone, that's even better. Regardless, the key is to find a time and place where, in the silence, he can hear God's voice and let the Holy Spirit lead him to the understanding and insights necessary for preaching on the selected Scripture passages. If he can do that, he's more than half way to where he needs to be.

## Method

Every preacher has some sort of method for preparing homilies. But not all methods are created equal. The bad ones, however they may differ in the specifics, all have certain things in common: They are rushed. They don't involve enough listening, either to God or other people. They lack adequate support. And they involve insufficient amounts of practice.

Similarly, the good ones, however they differ in specifics, also have certain things in common: They are not rushed. They involve lots of listening, depend upon the right amount of support, and include plenty of practice. Those are the four essential ingredients to any successful method of preparation. If any one of them is missing, something is almost guaranteed to be missing from the homily as well.

As for specific methods, the bishops have outlined one in *Fulfilled in Your Hearing*. Other authors of homiletics textbooks have outlined variations of their own. The method I use and the method I teach my seminarians to use for the preparation of their Sunday homilies is a combination of the bishops' and others I've read about over the years. It's simpler than most, but in its simplicity seems to lie the key to its effectiveness.

In essence, it's a seven day formula.

|  |  |
|---|---|
| *Sunday* | That evening, after the last Mass of the day has been said, read over the Scriptures for the following Sunday. |
| *Monday* | Read over the Scriptures for a second time and start praying over them. |
| *Tuesday* | Begin to exegete the text. Look for what personal message Christ is communicating. Here an encounter with Christ through the Scriptures must occur. "The |

homilist should rely on the presence of the Risen Lord within him as he preaches; a presence guaranteed by the outpouring of the Spirit that he received in ordination."[1] The homilist should not move forward with his preparation unless he is certain that his heart is burning within because Christ "spoke to him on the way and opened the Scriptures," like the disciples in the Emmaus narrative (Lk. 24: 26–27).

*Wednesday* Go to the commentaries. Study the translations of certain words and what they meant in their original language. Look for what the saints and scholars have said about the text over the years. If it's helpful, read homiletic aids that relay stories related to the specific passages of Scripture.

*Thursday* Write the homily. Some like to write more than others, but typically the more one writes, the more coherent and organized the homily will be.

*Friday* Start saying the homily out loud. Practice, if possible, in the empty church.

*Saturday* Practice some more. After delivering it for the first time on Saturday evening, look through it again and make any adjustments that can improve it for Sunday morning.

In addition to the steps outlined above, it's always helpful to talk over the readings with others early in the week. One way to do this is to begin Monday or Tuesday meetings with staff and volunteers by reading or paraphrasing the Scripture passages for the next Sunday and asking the attendees at the meeting to give some input on how those Scriptures speak to them. In doing so, the priest can get a better sense of how the readings connect with the people—how they touch them or seem relevant to them.

Throughout the process, a great deal of prayer also helps.

*Fulfilled in Your Hearing* says that to preach a homily is not so much to preach *on* the Scriptures, as it is to preach *through* the Scriptures.[2] It's letting God speak through the Scriptures to a specific group of people at a specific moment in time. But the priest can't communicate what he hasn't received. He has to encounter God in the Scriptures first. He has to discern what they're saying to him. He has to, in a sense, "name the grace," hearing God's voice speak to the present moment.

Whether the priest is reading the Scriptures, studying the commentaries, or writing out the words he plans to speak, every step of homily preparation should begin with prayer, end with prayer, and be conducted with a sense of God's presence. God has to be invited into the process so that he can guide the process.

It's also important to never underestimate the importance of a regular holy hour to the homily preparation process. The more faithful a priest is to that hour, the more it will enrich the other hours of the day. During adoration, God can speak to the priest as he reflects on the subject of his upcoming homily. And after the hour is over, that line of communication will remain open, directing and shaping his thoughts as he continues to work on his homily. In the life of a priest, contemplation must always precede proclamation. And there is no better place to learn the art of contemplation than in front of the Blessed Sacrament.

The last component to an effective method of homily preparation is taking the time to study. Not only is it important for the priest to draw upon biblical commentaries, but it's also important for him to cultivate an ongoing habit of serious study. He regularly needs to read theology, philosophy, Church history, lives of the saints, and cultural commentaries, growing in his understanding of God's Word, God's Church, and God's people. His seminary studies will never be enough. His graduate studies will never be enough. There is always more to learn and more to understand. And as the priest learns and understands more, he will find more personal fulfillment in his vocation and more new and relevant ways of communicating truth to the people he serves. He'll be able to make more connections, illustrate concepts more clearly, and flesh out meanings with greater precision and clarity. He'll build for himself a wealth of support from which he can draw, and, in turn, hand on to others.

Does this process, from start to finish, take a great deal of time? On one level, yes. Although every homily is different—some readings are easier to interpret and connect, others less so—a priest can expect to spend anywhere from seven to ten hours preparing a Sunday homily. If he can devote more time to it, even better.

But, for as lengthy of a process as that may seem, it's really not. In the long run, devoting an hour or so each day to homily preparation can actually save time. Putting off preparation until the weekend often costs priests dearly, both in the energy wasted by stress and in the hours some devote to last minute "cramming." Plus, the more a priest prioritizes the homily, the more it becomes a part of him. It ends up feeling not like an external duty, something he "has to do," but rather like a spiritual exercise, something that feeds him and gives him life. It becomes for him, as well as for the people to whom he preaches, an encounter with grace.

## THE HOMILY

### Structuring the Sunday Homily

The most important moment for the homilist doesn't come at the end of the homily. Nor does it come in the middle. The most important moment is the very beginning. It's the first sentence out his mouth and the first minute in which he preaches. In that moment, the men and women sitting in front of him decide if they're going to pay attention or if they're going to let their minds wander to the fight they had with their spouse before Mass or the meal they'll prepare when they return home. Stopping those minds from wandering is no easy feat. Not in a culture that is visual, not oral, and that subjects people to a constant barrage of information delivered in flashy packages and bite-sized pieces.

Accordingly, it's not generally best to begin a homily with the words, "In today's readings, we hear ..." There is, of course, a place in every homily for summations and signposting. It's just not at the very beginning.

Instead, a priest can begin with an attention-getting question that sums up the main point of his homily: "Why does marriage matter?" "Why does God permit us to suffer?" "What does God think about *American Idol*?" The more succinct the question and the more it conveys the heart of the homily, the better.

He can also begin with a statement that startles or intrigues: "In the kingdom of God, bigger is not better." "God know how to manage your time better than you."

Best of all, he can begin with a story. He can talk about a specific moment or human experience where the lesson of the day's reading was lived or made clear. He can talk about people and events that he's known and experienced, or he can draw on people and events from the larger culture. He can go back in time and tell a story from the past or he can make an analogy that points to the future. All can work equally well. The key is to find a moment that's relatable and accessible—something that people can connect with.

Once the preacher has people's attention, he can then turn towards the Scriptures and explain what they say to the question posed or event described. Sometimes he may want to give a little historical context. At other times, it may help to explain a particular word, offering a more precise meaning than the New American Bible conveys. The goal here is to illuminate the Scriptures, to deepen people's understanding of what they've just heard, so they can hear what God says through the readings more clearly.

A Sunday homily, however, can't end there. The preacher next needs to open up the lesson, connecting the readings back to the larger question at hand. Sometimes, this connecting may take a catechetical bent, explaining the Church's teaching on the specific doctrinal issue in question. If the second reading was Ephesians 5, a brief catechesis on marriage or the theology of the body would be appropriate. If the Gospel was taken from John 6, a catechesis on the Real Presence is possible. The Church's liturgical calendar and the lectionary's complementary passages also provide ample opportunities for catechesis on the Trinity (Trinity Sunday), the kingdom of God (Christ the King), the Marian dogmas (the feasts of the Motherhood of God, the Annunciation, the Ascension, and the Immaculate Conception), as well as on the Apostles, Church doctors, the saints, and more.

Regardless of whether or not the readings lend themselves to a catechetical moment, the homilist still needs to illustrate his main point, not just state it. He needs to support it, make it clear, and draw it out. He can do this with stories from real life, classic works of art and literature, or contemporary culture. He can quote Church documents or the writings of spiritual authors. He can point to what other commentators have to say. Whatever supporting material helps him make his point belongs here.

As the priest moves toward his conclusion, he has to make explicit how the particular lesson applies to his listeners. What is God asking them, as individuals and as a community, to do? What is required of them? And how can they begin to do what is required? He should be able to summarize the point of that lesson in one, brief sentence. And if he can't, it's likely his listeners won't grasp the point either.

Finally, whenever possible, the conclusion of a homily needs to help people make the transition to the Liturgy of the Eucharist. It needs to point them to the altar. At times, that pointing can be explicit, a direct reference connecting the lesson to what is about to happen in the Eucharist. At other times, that transition might be implicit. A moving homily on the virtues and our inability to practice them without supernatural assistance can stir up an awareness and a desire for the graces of Holy Communion. However the homily ends, it needs to move the listeners forward, filled with greater gratitude, love, and hope, as well as a greater desire to do God's will. The last minute needs to inspire, just as the first minute needs to intrigue. It also needs to be clear and direct, an obvious and crisp conclusion delivered head-on with no wandering and false stops. The more "false" conclusions a homily has, the more congregants will tune out before the final moments.

This structure isn't a hard and fast formula. On some occasions different components need more time and attention. On other occasions the components need to be rearranged or supplemented with other goals. But in the end, whenever possible, every homily should be structured in such a way that three basic questions are answered: 1) What does this have to do with me? 2) What do you want me to do? 3) What's in it for me if I do it?

If those three questions are answered, the listeners will understand the relevance of God's Word, in Scripture and Tradition. They'll grasp that God asks something of them and know what they need to do to answer him. They'll also understand why answering him matters. They'll discover that their answer is part of what will lead them to the happiness, peace, joy, and meaning for which they've been looking.

The trick, of course, is doing all this in seven to ten minutes. That's the ideal length today of the Sunday homily. Once upon a time, priests preached much longer. But that was before two generations of bad homilies pre-programmed people to stop listening as soon as the homily began. That was also before the advent of the Information Age and the ensuing crisis of attentiveness it created. Even the most attentive listeners' minds now usually start to wander after ten minutes.

Priests also need to consider families with small children. When the homily is too lengthy, that stretches out the length of the Mass in general. The longer the Mass, the more likely the youngest members of the parish will grow restless and disruptive. And the more restless and disruptive they become, the less anyone—parents or those around them—will enjoy being at church.

Priests have to remember that the homily is not a lecture. It's not a stand alone event. Occasionally, in certain times and places, it's possible to preach longer. But those times and places are relatively few, and unless a homilist is blessed with such an opportunity (e.g. preaching a Sunday Mass at a Catholic university or the main liturgy of a Catholic conference), it's best to aim for brevity. The goal is to leave them wanting more, not silently begging God to make the homily end.

## A Note on Weekday Homilies

Sunday homilies are something of a different breed from weekday homilies. They require more time, more preparation, and more supporting materials. They are the primary occasion for the proclamation of the Gospel in parish life. But weekday homilies are still homilies, and the priest owes it to God and the community gathered to prayerfully prepare for preaching. Some priests will devote an hour to preparing for a weekday homily. Some more. Most much less. The key to keeping preparation time brief without sacrificing quality is to keep the homily simple and keep the homily short.

In a weekday homily, the priest has time to do just one thing. He can reflect on the Scriptures. He can comment on an issue Christ addressed in the Gospel or a person mentioned in the readings. Occasionally it might be important to mention the saint of the day or a feast the Church is celebrating and connect that to the readings. The goal is to pass on one main insight that gives the congregation food for thought.

As for time, four minutes is generally the maximum amount of time a priest should allot to a weekday homily. Part of the reason for that brevity is the preacher. Rarely does he have the time necessary for preparing a long homily for every weekday Mass, and again, to preach too long without adequate preparation is never a good idea. The homily will end up lacking clarity and adequate support.

Another significant reason for brevity is parishioners' schedules. Although many attendees at a weekday Mass will be retirees, with no set schedule, a significant number will also be men and women on their way to or from work. If the Mass is offered mid-day, many will have given up their lunch hour to attend. Others will be mothers, and increasingly many will be homeschooling families taking a quick break from the work of the day. For them, as well as for the preacher, quick and concise homilies are best.

## DELIVERING THE HOMILY

### Rhetorical Skill

A homilist doesn't have to be a skilled rhetorician in order to preach effectively. He simply has to keep a few basic points about public speaking in mind.

First, he needs to speak clearly and at the right pace, neither too slow (which translates as sleepy) nor too fast (losing the congregation in his rush to fit everything in). He needs to change his tone and intonation regularly, and he needs to speak as he normally would, with no affectation.

The homily should essentially have the feel of a formal conversation. It shouldn't be chatty or overly casual, but it still should feel personal and natural. To ensure that everyone is a part of that conversation, the preacher needs to address his remarks to the people in the last pews in the Church, speaking a little more loudly than he normally would in order to reach those far back and those who don't hear well. Being comfortable with the microphone will help with that. So will practice.

Just as he gauges his volume to the congregation, so too should he gauge his language. His words should be simple. No one wants to bring a dictionary with them to the church in order to understand what Father is saying. His sentences should likewise be varied, their length and rhythm changing with no set pattern. Again, that acts as a check against the soporific effect.

Although it can be difficult to make eye contact from the pulpit, priests can achieve the effect of eye contact by picking out certain points in the church—a pillar, a pew, a corner—and speaking to those points. The more a preacher looks out into the congregation, the less free people feel to let their eyes wander off him and up towards the adorable baby in the pew in front or down towards the bulletin in their hands.

Gestures and carriage are also important. Gestures are good and necessary, but the wrong gestures, ones which feel forced or unnatural, can leave the congregation feeling like their priest just finished a Saturday seminar on public speaking at the Toastmaster's Club. Accordingly, when preaching, a priest should use the gestures he uses when he interacts with people outside the Church. He can shrug his soldiers, wave his hands, shake his head—pretty much whatever he does when he speaks in a parish meeting he can do in a homily. He also wants to stand up straight, never folding his arms or putting them behind his back. The trick is to be comfortable in one's own skin. If that has been achieved, the rest will follow.

As for where a preacher should deliver the homily, the pulpit is perhaps the best but not the necessary place. There is something very sacred about speaking from the pulpit, and standing there gives the priest a particular authority that standing on the sanctuary steps does not. Moreover, the pulpit is the safest choice. When a homilist stands behind the pulpit, he can't trip over his microphone cord or slip on the steps leading into the sanctuary. He can't awkwardly pace back and forth or up and down, and he never gets too close to anyone for their own comfort. He also remains at all times in the direct line of sight of the congregation, not proceeding so far up the center aisle that the people in the front pews have to crane their necks to see him.

Despite what some might say, descending into the congregation does not necessarily make people pay closer attention. Some people feel like their personal space is being violated and mentally back off from the preacher, actively, rather than merely passively, tuning him out in their discomfort. And nobody can pay attention for long to someone's back, which is what happens when priests move down the center aisle.

In the end though, it's not really a question of "where," but rather "how." Some are more comfortable and effective preachers without the pulpit in front of them. As long as they're careful not to make any of the mistakes outlined above, preaching from the sanctuary steps can be a fine alternative to the pulpit.

Lastly, it's important to have as little connection to the written text as possible. Although it's helpful for the preacher to write out the homily, it's rarely helpful to deliver the homily by reading what's written. If he is more comfortable with a fully-written out homily in front of him, a priest needs to do a great deal of work to make sure he's not relying on it. Typically, a preacher is more engaged with the congregation if he just has his outline and the necessary quotes and facts written down.

Some priests and deacons come by these skills naturally. They are born public speakers and those skills translate well into preaching. Others have to work at it. The key is practice, preaching homilies as many times as possible in empty churches, in front of mirrors, and even to a dog if there happens to be one about the rectory. Sometimes taping oneself is an effective way to discover verbal and physical tics that work their way into one's preaching. Asking friends or fellow preachers for their input can also be helpful.

And again, preparation matters. When a preacher has given ample time to his homily, when he's spent an entire week thinking about it, praying about it, and practicing it, he's much more free to deliver it with clarity and force than when he just begins working on it late Friday night. Familiarity breeds confidence, and confidence breeds effectiveness.

## Preaching on Difficult Subjects

Preaching about pornography is never easy. Defending the Church's teachings on marriage is always daunting. Challenging people to live the Church's teachings on sexuality can be downright panic-inducing. But now more than ever, homilies need to tackle these topics. If they don't, some parishioners will never hear or understand what the Church has to say about these things, nor will they know why she says what she does. When priests stay silent on these topics, the majority of their parishioners' views will be shaped by the culture, not the Church.

Preaching on these topics really isn't the question. The question is how. And "how" starts with staying positive and not going negative. Everything the Church teaches, she teaches for our good. God's laws are positive, making men free for happiness. All her teachings are beautiful. They are true. They offer people a way of life that leads to happiness and peace, now and in eternity. Accordingly, as much as possible, priests need to focus on that. They need to focus on the beauty of God's design for marriage and sexuality, the glory of the gift of life, the dignity of the human person. When an action does need to be condemned (such as using pornography or profligate spending), condemn the action, not the people doing the action, and root the explanation for the Church's condemnation of those behaviors in the violence they do to the person. Always connect how violating certain norms leads to unhappiness, while obeying them leads to happiness. The Church is so often depicted by the culture as the Church of no. Priests need to reject that characterization by highlighting the true yes that the Christian life actually is.

It's also important to have the facts straight. If a priest cites a study about the effectiveness of Natural Family Planning, he needs to have that study in front of him so that he doesn't misquote it. He likewise needs to know what the Church documents have to say and which Scripture passages support his argument. No one can tackle difficult subjects off the cuff. Everyone needs to do their homework. If not, people will challenge the preacher, and if he fails to meet that challenge, his credibility will diminish.

Finally, homilists need to remember to be sensitive to their congregation. At every Mass there will be adults capable of handling a direct discussion of human sexuality. But there will also be small children and teenagers. Parents work hard to protect their children's innocence. Most don't want their seven-year-olds to know details about homosexuality or pornography. They want to be the ones to speak to them about sex outside of marriage. That doesn't mean the priest shouldn't speak on those issues when children are present. There's no avoiding that. But he does need to be careful with his choice of words, speaking in such a way that he won't shock young children or unduly upset their parents.

❦

People are looking for truth. They're looking for meaning. They're looking to live full and happy lives. The culture isn't giving them that. That is why they've come to Mass. The nuts and bolts of a homily—the tools of construction—aren't what the average person in the pew thinks about when a priest steps up to preach. They're thinking about the message, the teaching, the wisdom the preacher has to give. They're thinking about what the homily has to say to them. If those pieces aren't in place, it doesn't matter how articulate or engaging the preacher is. Whether the people realize it or not, he won't be giving them what they need.

Homilies need to be clear, engaging, well structured, well prepared, and well spoken, in order for people to receive them. The packaging matters. It's how the message gets delivered. Use the wrong tools in the wrong way, and no matter how sure the foundation or how good the design, the whole thing will fall apart.

And that's something we cannot afford to have happen again.

## Conclusion
## Prophets On the Threshold

The Old Testament prophets were a motley crew. Isaiah, Jeremiah, Elijah, Elisha, and all their ilk roamed the hills and valleys of ancient Israel speaking truth to the wayward and the faithful alike. There often seemed no accounting for their actions—who they healed, who they fed, who they comforted. And the words that poured forth from them— proclamations of judgment and promises of restoration—seemed equally arbitrary. One minute they were cursing God's chosen people, raining down condemnation on their faithless hearts. The next minute they were blessing them, consoling the lost with all the tender love of a young mother.

But in the end, there was nothing arbitrary about the prophets. Where they went, what they said, how they said it: all flowed from a deep, abiding, intimate relationship with God. They looked to him. They listened to him. And in that looking and listening they saw what he wanted them to see and heard what he wanted them to hear. They received his vision. They saw the world with his eyes. They saw reality as he sees it. And their prophetic preaching arose out of that. They stood on the threshold of heaven and earth, party to a sacred conversation initiated by the Lord God, and they shared all they received with the people in their care.

That conversation, that preaching was possible, not simply because the prophets preached on the threshold, but because they lived on the threshold. Their prophetic task wasn't a job. It was a calling. A way of life. They were prophets, chosen and consecrated to a sacred mission. They couldn't not hand on what they received from God. That handing on defined them. And upon what they had to give, the salvation of a people depended.

God isn't asking priests today to wander about the countryside unshaven and unkempt, sleeping on the ground and feeding on locusts. But he is asking them to live like the prophets of old on a deeper level. He calls them to live on the threshold, seeing his vision and hearing his Word. He calls them to preach and minister to the wayward and the faithful, the lost and the found, those inside the Church and outside the Church. And when they are attentive, he gives them all they need to do just that. But they must be attentive.

Priests must be attentive to their history. They must know what God's vision for the Church in the modern world is, as well as why and how that vision has been subverted. They also must be attentive to the signs of the time, understanding the struggles, needs, and hopes of the people to whom they preach. And they must be attentive to the liturgy, sensible to the truth and beauty of the sacred prayer that is home to the Catholic homily.

When preachers are attentive to all that, they can structure their liturgical preaching according to the mind of the Church—evangelizing, catechizing, inspiring, and guiding people to God's desired end for them. They also can live as God would have them live, a rightly ordered soul imbuing their preaching with greater force and credibility. The consistent application of sound homiletic principles and tools to their preaching then becomes the glue or the thread, which binds all the other pieces together, connecting them into a coherent and effective whole.

That's what the reform of the reform means for homiletics. It is a reintegration of all that the Fathers of Vatican II intended for the Church into liturgical preaching. It is a preaching that is informed by the liturgy, by Scripture, by Tradition, by culture, by all the needs, perceived and unperceived, in the Catholic congregation. It learns from the past, draws on the present, and looks to the future. It is the proclamation of the faith—fully, faithfully, courageously, lovingly. It is an articulation of the yes that is the Christian life.

When a homily clearly and truly articulates that yes, it can become a game-changing moment. It can change individual lives and parishes, as well as the Church and the culture. It can awaken faith, deepen it, and form it. It can inspire the faithful to grow in wisdom and knowledge and help them to live as the Fathers of the Second Vatican Council hoped they would live, as, in fact, God wants them to live: as missionaries in the marketplace and apostles in the home.

A homiletics shaped by the reform of the reform is, itself, a key part of bringing about the reform of the reform. It is a key part of helping Catholics understand their role in the world. It nourishes the priesthood, nourishes the liturgy, and nourishes Catholic life. It helps makes possible all that Vatican II strove to give the Church.

Still, it can only help. Alone it can't do any of that. It too is simply one part of a greater whole—a whole made up of the Sacred Liturgy, the sacraments, religious education, youth ministry, adult faith formation, Catholic family life, and corporal works of mercy. All are essential parts of forming the faithful and feeding the hungry. Neglect any one, and the whole suffers. But in the grand scheme of things, the homily still holds a central place. It sets the tone for the proclamation of the faith outside the Mass. It also reveals or conceals the actualization of the faith taking place within the Sacred Liturgy. Upon it, so much depends.

## A Moment of Opportunity

When it comes to the life of the Church today, it's often easy to look at the glass as being half empty. There is so much bad news about the Church, so many damaging stories and so many barbed attacks. The statistics on Catholic faith and life are equally grim. We can't forget those stories or gloss over those statistics. They are all too real, and if we do forget or gloss over them, we run the risk of forgetting why and to whom we preach. We run the risk of losing perspective. But, and this is a very big "but," priests must not see those stories and statistics as simply a sketch of the obstacles they face in proclaiming the Gospel. They mustn't, no matter how easy or tempting it is, look at the glass as being half empty. They must see this moment in the life of the Church as one of the greatest opportunities in her history.

Not since the days of lions and gladiators has there been such a glaring need for the proclamation of the Gospel. Not in our lifetime, nor in the lifetime of the centuries of priests who came before us, has it mattered quite so much what the priest does with the seven to ten minutes that follow the proclamation of the Gospel. Those seven to ten minutes are an opportunity that moguls in Hollywood would pay millions for. They are an opportunity that Madison Avenue executives would sell their first born to have. In those seven to ten minutes, faith can be awakened, hearts stirred, minds transformed. In those seven to ten minutes, people can hear the voice of God speaking to them, consoling them, directing them, loving them. In those seven to ten minutes, everything can change.

But all that depends on the priest living and preaching from the threshold, just like the prophets of old. From there he must see, and from there he must speak. It's not enough for his homily to be that to which the reredos pointed—a sacred conversation. The priest himself must be a living reredos, a walking, talking, breathing sign of the sacred conversation taking place between heaven and earth. He must hear what God wants him to hear and speak what God wants him to speak. He must submit himself to the words of Christ in John 16:13. "He will not speak on his own authority, but whatever he hears he will speak." It is God's grace that ultimately makes all liturgical preaching effective. The rest is simply the best means of being open to and receiving that grace.

And the grace must be received. When it is, no lepers may be cured or widows' sons raised from the dead, but something just as miraculous will occur: Souls will find life, eternal life, and find it abundantly.

# Afterword

BY BISHOP DAVID A. ZUBIK
*Diocese of Pittsburgh*

As I read Father Joe Mele's engaging and challenging discussion of homiletics, I couldn't help but think of the "Nones." The "Nones" are a recent discovery of researchers. They are those in America who are neither atheist nor agnostic, but are not believers nevertheless. They are those folks who do not identify with any religious affiliation, attach little importance to religion in their lives, attend religious services only when dragged along to a baptism, wedding or funeral. That's why they are called "Nones."

They represent about 14 percent of the U.S. public and are distinct from complete non-believers in that many of them do have a vague belief in God, classify themselves in some way as spiritual, and one-in-five admits to praying on a daily basis, though it is unclear to whom or for what their prayers are directed.

That said, the lack of religious identity is clearly cross generational. Many people, now in their 70s, 60s, 50s, 40s or 30s, lost to faith in their early adulthood, have too often made a decision—without much thought—that lasts a lifetime. They create a life mired in post-modern secularism and consumerism.

Which brings me back to Father Mele's book. The "Nones" were created in our parishes and in our families. They were the children of believers—possibly marginal believers, but believers nonetheless—who never caught it, or caught it and dropped it by the wayside as they entered their young adult years.

Father Mele's book is for those who preach the New Evangelization to a targeted audience that we rarely think about when we use that term. Our evangelization efforts cannot be limited to those who have left the Church, and to the unChurched who have never experienced the faith other than through a Christmas carol on the radio or an Easter egg hunt.

Our New Evangelization must also be aimed squarely at not taking for granted those already in our Church, those already in the pews on Sunday. They can be future saints; or they can be future "Nones" or the parents of future "Nones." What Father Mele sees so clearly is that the art of homiletics in recent decades fell on hard times. Homiletics too often lost its evangelistic bent and "the nature of truth itself, in all its absoluteness, was diminished in the very place where it was supposed to be proclaimed."

"Homilies that do not teach, do not engage, do not challenge, and do not lead people to an encounter with the Eucharistic Christ" do not necessarily cause the existence of the "Nones," but they do not do anything to prevent them either. Father Mele calls for a "reform of the reforms" spelled out in the Second Vatican Council and shows us how to apply them to preachers with the goal of generating holiness; with the goal of leading people to Eternal Life.

This is the New Evangelization at work in our parishes.

Yes, we need the outreach and engagement programs with the culture.

Yes, we need to find those who have drifted away.

Yes, we need to invite the unChurched to join us.

But in doing so, we cannot forget those in our pews each Sunday. "Priests can no longer assume that everyone sitting in the pews on Sunday knows Christ," Father Mele warns. "Many don't. Many have never encountered him. They don't know they're called to have a personal, loving relationship with him. They don't know what that relationship entails. They likewise have never heard about the universal call to holiness. They have a vague notion about God and religious obligation, but not much else."

The work of evangelization—the New Evangelization—has to be done in every parish.

There is a story about Joe DiMaggio, the New York Yankee great. DiMaggio was once asked why he tried so hard every baseball game, and every at-bat in every baseball game. DiMaggio answered that at any game on any given day might find someone seeing their first ball game, someone who had bought a ticket that day and might be the first and only time ever to see him play. "I can't let that person down," DiMaggio explained.

That's how we must be with our preaching. We can't let people down! More so, we can't let Christ down! We have to preach each day as if it were:

- the first, last or only chance to call a person back;
- the first, last or only chance to make the faith come alive in their heart;
- the first, last or only chance to save their soul.

We have the task now of reaching out to the "Nones."

We have to find them.

We have to speak to them.

We have to give them back faith, hope and charity.

At the same time, we have to make certain that each week we are reaching out as well to those in our very midst who are drifting; those in our midst who are closer to the "Nones" than to believers.

My friend, Father Joe Mele, has spelled out how we can do that. Thanks, Joe, for the challenge. Thanks, Joe, for the book.

# NOTES

## Introduction

1  Timothy H. Sherwood, *The Preaching of Archbishop Fulton J. Sheen* (Lanham, MD: Lexington Books, 2010), ix.

2  James Brieg, "What U.S. Catholic Readers Think About Sermons," *U.S. Catholic*, no. 48, Nov. 1983, 6–18. Dennis Burke, "Why Priests Can't Preach," *Commonweal*, Vol. 122, No. 7 (Commonweal Foundation, April 7 1995), 15–18; Msgr. Charles Pope, "What do you think of Catholic Preaching?" March 17, 2010, http://blog.adw.org.

3  The CARA Report, 2012, p. 21, http://cara.georgetown.edu/CARAServices/requestedchurchstats.html.

4  A 2009 Gallup poll concluded that more Catholics approve of embryonic stem cell research than non-Catholics (63 percent versus 52 percent). A 2012 poll by the Public Interest Research group showed an even wider margin in the area of same-sex marriage (59 percent versus 52 percent). Similar disparities have been found regarding the issues of divorce, pre-marital sex, and homosexual behavior. See Dan Gilgoff, "Catholics the Same or More Liberal than Others on Moral Issues," *U.S. News & World Report* (March 30, 2009), http://www.usnews.com/blogs/god-and-country/2009/03/30/gallup-poll-catholics-the-same-or-more-liberal-than-others-on-moral-issues.html; http://www.gallup.com/poll/117154/catholics-similar-mainstream-abortion-stem-cells.aspx; and http://publicreligion.org/research/2012/05/research-note-evolution-of-american-opinion-on-same-sex-marriage/.

5  Second Vatican Council, Constitution on the Sacred Liturgy *Sacrosanctum concilium,* no. 34.

6  Vittorio Messori, Joseph Ratzinger, *The Ratzinger Report: An Exclusive Interview on the State of the Church* (San Francisco: Ignatius, 1985), 37–40.

## Chapter 1

1　Peter Hebblethwaite, *Pope John XXIII: Shepherd of the Modern World* (New York: Doubleday, 1985), 433.

2　Ibid., 48.

3　Marcellino D'Ambrosio, "Ressourcement Theology, Aggiornamento, and the Hermeneutics of Tradition," *Communio*, vol. 18, no. 4 (1991).

4　Xavier Rynne, *Vatican Council II* (Maryknoll, NY: Orbis Books, 1999), 513.

5　George Weigel, *Witness to Hope: The Biography of John Paul II* (New York: Harper Perreniel, 2005), 153.

6　Bill Huebsch, *Vatican II in Plain English: The Council* (Allen Texas: Thomas More Press, 1997), 52.

7　For a more thorough treatment of Vatican II and its aftermath see: Dietrich von Hildebrand, *Trojan Horse in the City of God: The Catholic Crisis Explained* (Manchester, NH: Sophia Institute Press, 1967); Matthew Lamb and Matthew Levereing, ed. *Vatican II: Renewal Within Tradition* (Oxford: Oxford University Press, 2008); Ralph McInerney, *What Went Wrong with Vatican II* (Manchester, NH: Sophia Institute Press, 2008); Justin Cardinal Rigali, *Reliving Vatican II: It's All About Jesus Christ* (Chicago IL: Liturgy Trade Publications, 2007); Tracy Rowland, *Culture and the Thomist Tradition After Vatican II* (London: Routledge, 2003).

8　D'Ambrosio, *Communio*, vol. 18, no. 4 (1991).

9　Bernard Cooke, *Ministry to the Word and Sacraments: History and Theology* (Minneapolis, MN: Fortress Press, 1980), 288.

10　Pope John Paul II, "The Twenty-Fifth Anniversary of the Secretariat for Promoting Christian Unity: Address to the Roman Curia," 1985, no. 59.

11　Second Vatican Council, The Dogmatic Constitution on the Church *Lumen gentium*, no. 8; Second Vatican Council, Decree on Ecumenism *Unitatis redintegratio,* no. 3; Pope Paul VI, Declaration on the Relation of the Church to Non-Christian Religions *Nostra aetate* (October 28, 1965), no. 2.

## Chapter 2

1　"Internet 2009 In Numbers": http://royal.pingdom.com/2010/01/22/internet-2009-in-numbers.

2　Maggie Jackson, *Distracted: The Erosion of Attention and the Coming Dark Age.* (Amherst: Prometheus, 2008), 14.

3   Jackson 84–85; Mark Bauerlein *The Dumbest Generation: How the Digital Age Stupefies Young Americans and Jeopardizes Our Future* (New York: Penguin, 2008), 71–161.

4   Emily Stimpson, "Dioceses Resolve to Strengthen Catechist Formation," *Our Sunday Visitor*, Sept. 6, 2009. Available at http://www.osv.com/tabid/7622/itemid/5284/Dioceses-resolve-to-strengthen-catechist-formation.aspx.

5   See CARA Report 2012.

6   Pew Forum Report, "Republican Tea Part Supporters More Mellow," March 2011:   http://www.people-press.org/2011/03/03/section-3-attitudes-toward-social-issues/.

7   United States Conference of Catholic Bishops, *Fulfilled in Your Hearing: The Homily in the Sunday Assembly*, 6.

8   Emily Stimpson, "Dioceses Resolve to Strengthen Catechist Formation," *Our Sunday Visitor*, Sept. 6, 2009, available at http://www.osv.com/tabid/7622/itemid/5284/Dioceses-resolve-to-strengthen-catechist-formation.aspx.

9   Ibid.

10  James Wehner, *The Evangelization Equation: The Who, What, and How* (Steubenville: Emmaus Road, 2011), 11.


## Chapter 3

1   *Fulfilled in Your Hearing*, 17.

2   *Sacrosanctum concilium* 7; John Paul II, "On Active Participation in the Liturgy: Discourse of the Holy Father to the Bishops of the Episcopal Conference of the United States of America (Washington, Oregon, Idaho, Montana and Alaska)," October 9, 1998, 2, available at http://www.adoremus.org/JPIIadlim1198.html.

3   Joseph Ratzinger, *The Spirit of the Liturgy*, trans. John Saward (San Francisco: Ignatius Press, 2000), 21–22.

4   Ibid.

5   Ibid., 70.

6   See Scott Hahn, *The Lamb's Supper* (New York: Doubleday, 1999).

7   *Sacrosanctum concilium*, 9–10.

8   Scott Hahn, *Letter and Spirit* (New York: Doubleday, 2005), 86.

9   Ratzinger, *The Spirit of Liturgy*, 165.

10  Guido Marini, Address to the Year of Priests Clergy Conference, Jan. 6, 2010. Text available at http://www.newliturgicalmovement.org/2010/01/clergy-conference-in-rome-address-of.html.

11  *Fulfilled in Your Hearing*, 19.

12 United States Conference of Catholic Bishops, *Preaching the Mystery of Faith: The Sunday Homily*, 22.

## Chapter 4

1 Peter John Cameron, OP. Unpublished conference notes: *The Theology of Preaching and The Poetics of Preaching*, Preaching Workshop for Second and Third Year Theologians, Pontifical North American College (Rome, September 15–26, 1997), 98.
2 *Fulfilled in Your Hearing*, 20.
3 Ibid., 23.
4 Lineamenta, 35, XII Ordinary General Assembly. Available at http://www.vatican.va/roman_curia/synod/documents/rc_synod_doc_20070427_lineamenta-xii-assembly_en.html.
5 *Fulfilled in Your Hearing*, 18.
6 *Presbyterorum ordinis* 4.
7 *Evangeliuum vitae* 14; *Fulfilled in Your Hearing*, 20.
8 For example, see Joseph Ratzinger's December 12, 2000 "Address to Catechists and Religion Teachers." Available at http://www.ewtn.com/new_evangelization/Ratzinger.htm.

## Chapter 5

1 *Fulfilled in Your Hearing*, 1.
2 Francis Fernandez, *In Conversation With God: Lent and Eastertide* (New Rochelle, NY: Scepter Publishers, 1989), 433.
3 Karl Rahner, "Christian Living Formerly and Today," *Theological Investigation* 7, (London: Darton, Longman & Todd, 1975), 15.
4 Alcuin Reid, *Looking Again at the Question of Liturgy with Joseph Ratzinger* (Farnbrough, UK: St. Michael's Abbey Press, 2004), 105.

## Chapter 6

1 *Preaching the Mystery of Faith*, 22.
2 *Fulfilled in Your Hearing*, 20.